So We Do Not Lose Heart

Biblical Wisdom For All Our Days

Demetrius R. Dumm, O.S.B.

Archabbey Publications
Latrobe, Pennsylvania

Library of Congress Cataloging-in-Publication Data

Dumm, Demetrius, 1923-
   So we do not lose heart : biblical wisdom for all our days / Demetrius R. Dumm.
      p. cm.
   Includes index.
   ISBN 0-9773909-1-8 (pbk.)
      1. Older Catholics–Prayer-books and devotions–English. 2. Bible–Meditations. I. Title.

BX2170.A5D86 2006
242'.5--dc22

                              2006045419
                              CIP

Printed in the United States of America
Archabbey Publications
300 Fraser Purchase Road
Latrobe, Pennsylvania 15650-2690
http://www.stvincentstore.com

Cover photo and book design by Kimberley A. Opatka-Metzgar
Editorial Assistant, Sarah Yaple
Archabbey Publications

CONTENTS

PREFACE

The cover of this book has a symbolic as well as an historical meaning. Historically, it is a photograph of five of my grandnieces and grandnephews who are gathered in the cemetery of Saint Vincent Archabbey and Parish. They are children of my nephew, Pat, and his wife, Virginia, ranging in age from two to twelve. Their names are, from left to right, Adelaide, Nicholas, Carolyn, Benjamin and Stephen. They are typical children who are full of life and who do not at all feel threatened by the existence of cemeteries.

Symbolically, these children represent the ultimate victory of life in a society where death is feared and where the final victory of life seems to be little more than a fanciful dream. By contrast, these children are not at all concerned about the implication of the crosses and the tombstones in the cemetery where they are seated. In that respect, they are unwitting models for all of us who dare to dream of unending life through our union with Christ.

Our yearning for eternal life and happiness is also encouraged by the title of this book, which is taken from Paul's Second Letter to the Corinthians: "So we do not lose heart.

Even though our outer nature is wasting away, our inner nature is being renewed day by day" (4:16). Vibrant children in a cemetery remind us therefore, through all our days but especially as we grow older, that the horizons of human life are constantly illuminated by God's love for us, guaranteed by Jesus himself, who represents a resounding "Yes" to all God's promises, including especially the promise of life (see 2 Cor 1:20).

INTRODUCTION

When we were children, we felt very small and we yearned to be taller and stronger. I recall that my uncle visited our home one time when I was very young and he lifted me up to his eye-level. I could scarcely imagine that some day I would actually be able to see the world from that giddy height. I yearned to be "grown-up" so that I would no longer be "looked down upon" and "talked down to." At that time, I did not realize that being grown up also meant beginning to be old and that I would eventually be bent over from that height and then laid low—far lower in fact than I ever had been as a little child.

This rather frightening prospect has caused me to appreciate a new way of looking at the human experience. From a biblical perspective, this experience is not limited to the fortunes of a human mind and body. For St. Paul reminds us that our mortal bodies house a spiritual power that, if properly nurtured, can overcome all the limitations of our human condition. His words are exceedingly consoling: "So we do not lose heart. Even though our outer nature is wasting away, our inner nature is being renewed day by day" (2 Cor 4:16). This inner renewal begins with our baptism and provides the promise of continuous growth even as our lives become more and more fragile.

In many other passages also, the Bible is a wonderful resource for comfort and hope on our human journey. We believe that the Bible is the Word of God. It is, therefore, a message from the transcendent world about the meaning and purpose of our human existence in this limited world—a world that had a beginning and will someday come to an end.

The God who inspired the biblical authors and who guarantees the trustworthiness of their message is also the Creator of the universe. And no one knows better than the One who made the world what its true purpose is and what its true destiny will be. More importantly, the Creator also knows best what is expected of us human creatures who inhabit that world and what constitutes a successful and happy human life.

All of this is clearly spelled out in the pages of the Bible. For most of us, however, the Bible is a very large book and we scarcely know how to deal with it. We want to embrace it but it seems almost impossible to put our arms around it. We need, therefore, to discover which parts of the Bible are central to our quest for the meaning of human life...and death.

PATHWAYS TO FREEDOM

After reading and teaching and praying the Bible for more than fifty years, I have concluded that this wonderful book is primarily about God's love and our freedom. Our freedom comes ultimately from God's love because this loving Creator is the source of our experience of goodness and beauty and love in our lives, which in turn gives us the confidence and freedom to become loving, caring persons ourselves. It is true that we may choose not to love and that is called sin. But we may also choose to repent and thus to return to the path of love and kindness.

As we become friends with the Bible, we should expect to discover the interaction of love and freedom which is the primary message contained in those two great revelatory events that anchor respectively the Old and New Testaments. All of the Old Testament was written after, and in the light of, God's decisive act to liberate the Hebrew slaves from the bondage of the Pharaoh—an act that has come to be known as the Exodus. And the entire New Testament was written after, and in the light of, God's decisive act by which Jesus was raised from the dead, thus enabling us also to escape the ultimate bondage of sin and death. The passion, death and resurrection of Jesus, which occurred on the exact anniversary of the Exodus, is therefore the ultimate divine act of love and liberation in our history.

It is true that the Exodus of ancient Israel is described as a physical liberation from the terrible bondage of slavery, but there was also a deeper liberation which occurred in the minds and hearts of those Hebrew slaves. For they discovered, through the witness of Moses, a God who was not only powerful, like the Pharaoh, but also loving and gentle, which the Pharaoh was not. In a word, they discovered a God who loved them for themselves and not just for their productivity.

In this new experience, they also discovered that, since God used his perfect freedom to choose them, they must forever remember that the only legitimate use of freedom on their part is to love others so that they too may be free. In fact, I often wonder whether there will be need to ask more than one simple question at the final judgment, namely, Did you let my people go? Or were you like the Pharaoh who tried to control and manipulate others?

This divine kind of loving is unconditional. The highly civilized Egyptians were, humanly speaking, far more attractive than the Hebrew slaves, covered as they were with mud and bent over from carrying bricks. And yet God chose the Hebrew slaves. The only explanation is that true goodness is always attracted to need more than to beauty. Its purpose is to create beauty where it did not exist rather than simply to notice it and feast on it.

This revelation of God's love for us has become even more explicit in Jesus Christ, who is the very embodiment of God's love in our midst. His radical teaching that unselfish love is the only power that brings lasting freedom and happiness led to his own loving self-sacrifice. He lived the message he taught. Then the validity of his teaching was confirmed by God in the most dramatic fashion by his resurrection from the dead—a victory that reveals, once and for all, the standard for measuring success or failure in our own lives. Do we live by the wisdom of Jesus or do we choose another more convenient wisdom? Do we seek happiness through selfish indulgence or do we trust the divine promise that real happiness comes only from unselfish love? Indeed, loving others will require sacrifices, as we learn on the Good Fridays of our lives, just as it also leads to final freedom and joy, which we celebrate in our resurrection experiences.

THE MANY KINDS OF HUMAN BIRTH

The possibility of loving as Jesus does is determined by the quality of our freedom. This pathway to ever-greater freedom is marked by a series of new births. Physical or biological birth is only the first of many discoveries of new life, new worlds and new opportunities. The infant begins its journey in its mother's womb, but we count its birth from the moment when it leaves the nourishing and protective confines of the womb to greet a whole new world—a world that is at first strange and threatening but which soon becomes a source of wonderment. In those very early years, it seems that the child is "eating up" with wonder-filled eyes that amazing world that lies all around it. All of this amounts to a new psychological birth.

As time passes, the child learns about its own special place in this strange environment. All the while, this child is learning about names, like God and Jesus and Mary. It is taught to say simple prayers and it begins to notice the difference between good and evil. These are the first hints of an emerging religious sense and it signals a new birth into a spiritual world that is so much larger than the world of everyday life.

We must distinguish, however, between these first hints of spiritual birth, due mainly to the influence of believing parents, and a fully conscious and personal choice to claim in our own name what was promised by our sponsors at the time, usually distant, of our baptism. In the language of the liturgy, our sponsors promised for us that we "renounced Satan," and that we "believed in Jesus." At that time, of course, we were totally unaware of what any of this really meant.

Our real birth into the spiritual world usually comes after our early teens (and sometimes long after that), when we begin to ask ourselves whether we now understand and are truly committed to what was said for us by our baptismal sponsors many years before. This moment often provokes a crisis in the lives of young adults as they begin to question whether they can really embrace all that they have been told about faith and

God and the Church.

Very often, this crisis comes when young adults go away to college where they are challenged to think for themselves and where they may meet professors or fellow students who do not share their religious views. If students "lose" their faith in these circumstances, it may very well be that they have merely lost the faith that they have "borrowed" from their parents. In which case, they should recognize that they are now offered a precious opportunity to claim their baptismal faith in their own names. If this happens, they will understand for the first time what being born of God really means.

Such an adult decision will also illuminate the true meaning of their baptismal promises. Now they will be able to understand that renouncing Satan means rejecting the very attractive but misleading suggestion of Satan that happiness can be achieved by selfish and self-centered behavior. This is the big lie of the devil (a word that means "deceiver") and it is for this reason that Jesus referred to Satan as "a liar and the father of lies" (John 8:44). They will also declare their firm conviction of faith that it is only the way of Jesus—the way of unselfish love and compassion—that leads to true happiness and eternal life. This is not an easy choice because unselfishness usually means putting aside one's own interests in order to respond to the needs of others, and this can often be quite painful. Nonetheless, we are told, and experience bears it out, that this is the only way to be happy even in this life.

Such a free and mature decision is truly a new birth. In a sense, it awakens the seed planted in us at baptism and initiates a new life within us that has the potential to grow ever stronger even as our physical and psychic life begins to show the inevitable signs of aging and decline. Unfortunately, it is also possible to draw back from this commitment to unselfish and generous concern for others. In that case, the new spiritual life within us will be like a neglected child that grows weak and sickly for lack of care and nourishment.

NOURISHING SPIRITUAL LIFE

This image of spiritual malnutrition is most appropriate because it suggests that a superficial believer has begun to live in a way that contradicts the meaning of that primary Christian nourishment which is the Eucharist. As a sacrament of Body-broken and Blood-poured-out, the Eucharist demands of those who receive it a commitment to lay down their own lives for the sake of others. This commitment to unselfishness is also nourished by prayer by which we not only ask God to give us the strength to live unselfishly but also remind ourselves of what is most central to our lives and most likely to bring happiness.

In the best of circumstances, we will discover the full implications of our baptismal commitment and then make a clear and firm decision to make that commitment the guiding star of our lives. In fact, however, we usually come to an informed understanding of the implications of our baptismal birth only gradually. In most cases, there are years full of distractions and preoccupations, which may cause us to postpone our coming to terms with the challenge of that spiritual birth. Making a living and raising a family and surviving the ups and downs of life tend to interfere with the kind of focussed attention that is required for spiritual growth.

Nonetheless, our full understanding of the baptismal commitment to unselfish behavior and our generous embracing of that ideal clearly constitute the key to the spiritual life. This awareness will serve us well when we begin to confront the slow but inexorable reality of declining health and the loss of control that accompanies it.

BIBLICAL REFLECTIONS

The reflections that follow are intended to be reminders of the realistic but wonderfully hopeful wisdom of the Bible as we look for meaning and encouragement in the midst of weakness and decline. The Bible reminds us that it is a good and loving Creator who gives us our human life and who has determined that it should not last forever. And God speaks to us through the Scriptures when they assure us that this span of human life is really a precious opportunity for discovering a life that does not succumb to the power of death. This mortal life is, in other words, a glorious opportunity for discovering how to be born into a new and endless kind of life.

These reflections will be based on texts from the entire Bible. The texts chosen are only a sampling of the hundreds of passages that might have been selected. However, these texts do represent a broad sampling and touch upon most of the facets of our struggle to live and hope even as we grow old and face death. Most of all, they will remind us that old age need not be a time of sadness and frustration, much less despair.

The experience of Jesus in his public ministry will remind us that the fruitful activity of Galilee (our years of productivity) can give way to an even more fruitful period of loving trust and cheerful patience in Judea (our years of retirement). Our secular culture tells us, in a thousand subtle but unmistakable ways, that real life is about over when we retire from full-time employment, but the gospels tell us that these later years can be for us, as they were for Jesus, the most precious and fruitful time of our lives.

The reflections that follow are based then upon texts of the Bible that help us to deal with the challenges that face us when we reach middle age and beyond...which realistically means any time after forty! These reflections will not be concerned only with those relatively few texts that explicitly deal with the problems of aging. They will be concerned rather with the challenge of learning to trust when one begins to lose control, or with the readiness to hope when the future looks threatening, or with the prayerful nurturing of that spiritual child who is struggling to grow stronger within us.

In reflecting on these biblical texts, my intention is not to "explain" them in a way that attempts to "control" their spiritual message. My aim is rather to comment on them in a way that will release their power to give us encouragement and comfort when life begins to be more difficult. With that in mind, I will try to show great respect for these precious words even as I attempt to serve them by offering interpretations that speak to our experience as mortal and fragile human beings.

1

THE JOY THAT LIES AHEAD OF US

Therefore, since we are surrounded by so great a cloud of witnesses, let us also lay aside every weight and the sin that clings so closely, and let us run with perseverance the race that is set before us, looking to Jesus the pioneer and perfecter of our faith, who for the sake of the joy that was set before him endured the cross, disregarding its shame, and has taken his seat at the right hand of the throne of God. (Hebrews 12:1-2).

As we grow older and the future seems dark with threats, it becomes ever more difficult to maintain a positive and cheerful attitude about our lives. However, the author of the Letter to the Hebrews reminds us that we are not alone on this difficult journey. There is, first of all, that great multitude of people who have gone before us and who are so much a part of our lives that they are said to surround us on every side. These are not only the saints but also the many persons who have loved us and are still in touch with us even though they have gone ahead of us.

We are encouraged then to lay aside that heaviness and

helplessness that often weighs us down and to run, on nimble feet, the path that so many others have taken. This is a well-traveled path and there are so many wonderful people who have walked it. In other words, as we grow older and approach the end of our lives, we are in very good company. So many people whom we admire and love, such as, parents, teachers and dear friends, have taken this same path and await us with open arms. Surely this cannot be such a dangerous road to follow.

But most of all we look to "Jesus, the pioneer and perfecter of our faith." He has gone ahead of us and has blazed the trail for us. Someone has said that we should imagine that Jesus has gone ahead of us into the future and that, when we finish our journey, we simply "catch up" to him! What a joyful moment that will be, especially if we have become very close to Jesus in this life.

What we see in Jesus, as he made his journey, is not an experience that was exempt from the hardships of human life. Indeed, very few of us will ever be asked to endure anything approaching his agony. But the secret of Jesus' ability to endure the most severe trials was his conviction about "the joy that was set before him." He was able to endure present suffering because his future was bathed in the glory that comes from the totally reliable promises of his heavenly Father.

I have often thought that, if I were asked to summarize the entire Bible in one word, that word would be "promise." Indeed, everything in the Bible points toward the future and a true believer is not one who enjoys all kinds of satisfaction here but rather one who lives in promise. Jesus himself, as the promised Messiah, is at the center of this promise. As St. Paul says, we who believe are "marked with the seal of the promised Holy Spirit; this is the pledge of our inheritance toward redemption as God's own people" (Eph 1:13-14). And St. Paul also writes that in Jesus "every one of God's promises is a 'Yes'" (2 Cor 1:20).

Thus, God's promise that our faithfulness will be rewarded beyond our wildest dreams constitutes that "joy" toward which we move in the company of Jesus and all the saints. Moreover, the older we grow, the closer we are to that joy, in spite of present weakness and fear. There can be no question that our condition of weakness may make all this seem to be no more than "pie in the sky." But we must read those comforting words of Scripture over and over again until we drive all negative and discouraging thoughts out of our minds and thus allow God's promises to fill our being and illumine our path.

There is a wonderful passage in the First Letter of John that should be a constant reminder of the power of our God-given faith to overcome all obstacles: "And this is the victory that conquers the world, our faith" (5:4). It is, therefore, our faith in God's promises that gradually enables us to overcome all our fears and anxiety about the future as we begin to see a dawn of joy beyond the dark clouds.

When the First Letter of John tells us that our faith can conquer the world, he is reminding us that the world is a place where pessimism has the last word. The classic philosophy of secular culture is expressed in the sad command: "Eat, drink, be merry, for tomorrow you die!" This may make sense for the young and strong but it represents nothing but desperation and absurdity for those who grow older. It is this disastrous philosophy of hopelessness that is contradicted and "conquered" by our faith. For our faith puts us in touch with God who has assured us of a future that is better than any past could ever be.

2

WE ARE GOD'S BELOVED CHILDREN

In those days Jesus came from Nazareth of Galilee and was baptized by John in the Jordan. And just as he was coming up out of the water, he saw the heavens torn apart and the Spirit descending like a dove on him. And a voice came from heaven, "You are my Son, the Beloved; with you I am well pleased" (Mark 1:9-11).

The evangelist is not interested in giving us the exact date of the beginning of the public ministry of Jesus. The phrase, "in those days," is not very helpful to an historian. But we must remember that the gospel writer is not telling us about someone, like Napoleon or George Washington, who was perhaps very influential within the limits of human history. Rather, we are being introduced to a Savior who came to show people of all times and places how to live this earthly life in a way that will lead to eternal happiness. In that light, the exact date of the beginning of his ministry is almost irrelevant.

The account of the actual baptism is very brief. In fact, it comprises no more than one verse (see above). The interpretation of Jesus' baptism comes when we are told what happened after the actual baptism. For it is only when Jesus comes up out of the water that he sees the heavens "torn apart." This very strong statement suggests that God has been waiting for this special moment when Jesus will be standing with Israel pleading for the beginning of God's dramatic intervention to restore the fortunes of his chosen people. Thus, the heavens are being torn apart from God's side. The people who accepted the baptism of John were declaring their readiness for God's coming; now God in turn declares his readiness to act in their behalf. The rending of the heavens tells us how eager God is to respond to the presence of Jesus.

The presence then of the Holy Spirit, who appears in the form of a dove, tells us about the nature of God's imminent activity in human history. We recall that the Spirit hovered over the waters in the Genesis story of creation (1:1). And the dove that brought back the olive branch to Noah (Gen 8:11) was another symbol of a new world, a new creation. In the context of the baptism of Jesus, this means that something radically new is about to happen. Nothing will ever be the same again.

Finally, the words from heaven tell about the nature of this new creation. It will come about through an influx of divine love in the person of Jesus such as no one could have dreamed possible. The infinite love of God the Father will henceforth be concentrated in God's incarnate Son and, through him, will radiate to the whole world in a way that has the potential to transform everything. If that has not happened to date, it can only be that we human beings have not allowed this love to pass through us to touch and renew the world.

It is important to note that the baptismal experience of Jesus was not just a single episode in his life. Rather, it is clear that he heard those liberating and energizing words of his Father all through his ministry when he withdrew from his disciples to pray alone in some deserted place. He heard these comforting words most especially during his ordeal in the garden of Gethsemane.

This story of the baptism of Jesus is not meant for him alone. When we are baptized, we too hear the loving voice of God, saying, "You are my beloved child; I love you more than you will ever know." And, just as in the case of Jesus, these liberating words of love are being spoken to us every minute of every day in our lives! Too often, however, we are not listening.

To grow old gracefully, we must begin as soon as possible to listen in quiet prayer for these words of God, so that we too, like Jesus, may be strengthened every day to make the journey of life with him. In the leisure that comes with old age, it is so important that we take time to pray, to entertain the presence of God and to listen every day for these most important words in our lives: "You are my beloved child; I love you very much."

God will speak these words to our hearts and in a thousand quiet ways he will embrace us with his strength. As a consequence, we will be less impatient, more trusting and more peaceful. We will be able to maintain hope in the most distressing moments. And we will be comforted in our own Gethsemane as we await the victory of resurrection and glory. God usually speaks to us in whispers, but there is indomitable power in his words. Let us be sure to listen every day to this life-giving voice of God.

3

CHOOSING LIFE OVER DEATH

I call heaven and earth to witness against you today that I have set before you life and death, blessings and curses. Choose life so that you and your descendants may live, loving the LORD your God, obeying him, and holding fast to him… (Deut 30:19-20).

These words from the Book of Deuteronomy are presented as the last instruction of Moses to the Israelites as they are about to enter and take possession of the Promised Land. In that context, they remind the Israelites that success or failure usually depends upon one's ability to choose. No normal person chooses death and curses, of course, but that choice is made for us when we fail to choose life and blessings.

Choosing life and blessings is not as easy as one may think. Death and curses are everywhere and at times they are so dominant that it seems useless to oppose them. Choosing hidden goodness over dominant and prevalent evil is an act of both freedom and courage.

The freedom to choose comes from having been loved. There is no other source of freedom. With it comes confidence and a sense of identity. Some have experienced a great deal of love and their freedom is obvious. Others have been neglected, but even they have some experience of love and some beginnings of freedom. It is vitally important to accept loving—from relatives and friends, from the beauty of nature, from God—so that our lives can be our own. To be a slave is to have to ask someone else who we are.

Courage also is required when the choice for goodness and life is made in situations filled with violence and death. I think courage comes from a habit of little victories over evil. Courage can flourish where courage has been practiced and where it is cherished.

The words of Moses are most appropriate for the Israelites as they prepare to enter an unknown land and to face unknown dangers. God wants his people to know that he still loves them and that they must continue to trust in his goodness. He has brought them out of the land of Egypt and he can bring them safely into the Promised Land, but only if they remember and count on his enduring love for them.

These words of Moses are spoken to us also as we struggle to choose life and blessings in all the difficult situations of our lives. Sometimes death and curses seem almost too strong to resist. Health fails, friends die and our sinful nature asserts itself. But we can still choose life and blessings. Though this is difficult, it is far from impossible.

Sometimes, choosing life means simply refusing to give in to death. It means choosing to think about the reality of goodness—in God, in friends, in nature and, at least sometimes, in ourselves. It is true that we cannot prevent dark thoughts from invading our minds, but we can choose not to keep them there. And as we deliberately replace such thoughts with

remembrances of goodness and love we are also able to overcome gradually the power of that darkness in our lives.

As we grow older, the power of death becomes more obvious. But we also have had years to prepare for this confronta-
tion. Even as our joints ache and our eyesight grows dim, we
remember the experience of goodness in our lives and thus
discover a basis for hope, no matter what. As we enter the
unknown land of failing health, we are comforted and reassured by the words of Moses to Israel: "loving the LORD, your
God, obeying him, and holding fast to him…" (Deut 30:20).

Then Moses offers them the promise of God—a promise
that illuminates even the darkest future: "for that means life to
you and length of days, so that you may live in the land that
the Lord swore to give to your ancestors, to Abraham, to Isaac,
and to Jacob" (Deut 30:29). This Promised Land is the eternal
life for which we yearn and which God wishes us to have.

Sometimes we think that "eternal life" begins only when
this life comes to an end. But that is not the way the Bible
understands it. It is clear, especially in John's gospel, that the
seeds of eternal life are sown long before we die. This occurs
at baptism sacramentally, but it becomes a living reality only
when we begin to live the implications of our baptism. This
involves, first of all, the rejection of Satan's "big lie" that we
can achieve happiness by living for ourselves alone. Then,
and most importantly, we affirm the wisdom of Jesus by com-
mitting ourselves to unselfish behavior. This new, spiritual life
is meant to grow throughout life and it will then become our
real life as we finally let go of our physical life in death.

4

GOD SMILES ON US

It is you who light my lamp; the LORD, my God, lights up my darkness.... (Psalm 18:28).

Darkness has always been a source of fear and anxiety for us humans. It is so frightening because we cannot move in it for fear of stumbling or falling. It is frightening also because it seems to be the hiding place for all the forces of evil and violence and destruction. It is not just children who are afraid of a dark room.

Light, on the contrary, has always been a powerful and positive symbol in the history of God's people. When God said, on the first day of creation, "Let there be light" (Gen 1:3), he was expressing this symbolic meaning. If we have read the Genesis account of creation carefully, we must have wondered how there could have been light on the first day when the sun and moon and stars had not yet been created. The answer is clear when we realize that the author saw creation as a reflection of the liberation of his ancestors from the bondage of Egypt.

The Hebrew slaves had lived for some two hundred years

in the darkness and emptiness and nothingness of Egyptian oppression. Suddenly God delivered them and the first fruit (the "first day") of this deliverance was the light that represents symbolically their freedom and identity and self-worth. They could now "see" their lives as destined for more than drudgery and futility; they could finally see the bright horizon of hope and joy and peace.

The psalmist declares that it is God who lights up his lamp. The familiar lamp fueled by olive oil is no longer reliable because his eyes have grown dim and the darkness is closing in on him. But he is not alone; God, his friend, has become the light of his life.

This wonderful light that comes from God dispels even the thickest darkness and turns the night of human life into a day without shadows. The result is immediate and lasting: "The lord is my light and my salvation, whom shall I fear?" When we grow older, fear becomes a constant companion— fear of becoming dependent on others, fear of pain, fear of the unknown. But God is our light and our salvation. When that conviction takes hold in our minds and hearts, there is no longer any cause for fear.

This light that God provides for us even in the darkest night comes from the fact that his face is turned toward us in loving attention. "For he did not despise or abhor the affliction of the afflicted; he did not hide his face from me, but heard when I cried to him" (Psalm 22:24). We are so dependent on God's goodness and mercy that, should he turn his face away from us, we would immediately feel the cold and darkness; we would immediately begin to shiver and to shrivel up.

But the Bible assures us constantly that God does not wish to do that. It is we who are more likely to turn our faces away from God. When God chose to create us, he also promised to keep us in the warmth of his loving attention. We are programmed from the beginning to respond to that loving, smiling face of God as a sunflower responds to the sun and follows it across the sky.

It is true, of course, that it is only through the gift of faith that we can experience this blessing that comes from the smiling face of God. The gift of faith enables us to find the blessing in God's creation, but that is merely preliminary to finding the supreme blessing that comes from the beauty of God's face. When God smiles on us, we are truly liberated from the darkness in life and can smile back at God in worship and gratitude.

When we live in the sunshine of God's loving countenance, we are liberated from the paralysis that comes from fear and anxiety. The psalmist expresses this reality in graphic language. "He made my feet like the feet of a deer, and set me secure on the heights" (Ps 18:33). When we see a deer leaping effortlessly and yet safely over rocky terrain, we realize how slow and clumsy we are by comparison...and especially so if we are getting on in years.

Nonetheless, God's smile is so energizing that we can be, in spirit at least, as nimble and sure-footed as the most graceful deer. It is always a beautiful and comforting experience to come upon someone who, though advanced in years, still has that joyful exuberance that can come only from living in the warmth and joy of God's smiling face.

5

THE CROSS OF JESUS IS ALL ABOUT LOVE

For the message about the cross is foolishness to those who are perishing, but to us who are being saved it is the power of God.... We proclaim Christ crucified, a stumbling block to Jews and foolishness to Gentiles, but to those who are the called, both Jews and Greeks, Christ the power of God and the wisdom of God. For God's foolishness is wiser that human wisdom, and God's weakness is stronger than human strength (1 Cor 1:18, 23-25).

The greatest paradox of Christianity is the equal emphasis placed on both the cross and the resurrection. Both of these realities are absolutely essential to the meaning of Jesus. The cross is a terrible disappointment without the resurrection, just as the resurrection is pure fantasy without the cross. The cross means, therefore, that our hope of new life is grounded in the reality of our present mortality. And the resurrection means that there is a wondrous ending to our mortal existence if we learn how to seize the opportunity that God has given us.

When Paul says that the cross is "foolishness to those who are perishing," he means that it cannot be taken seriously by anyone who believes that all of human existence is limited to the time between birth and death. By contrast, those "who are being saved," that is, those who believe in the message of Jesus, are convinced that this present life is no more than a kind of antechamber to the fullness of life that God has planned for them. As Paul Harvey would say, they believe in "the rest of the story."

These two visions of human life are radically different and totally irreconcilable. Paul's great concern is that we may succumb to the temptation to try to live as if both were true. We do this when we become deeply immersed in the affairs of this world—building monuments and making money—and, at the same time, try to keep in touch with religion just in case the "bank" of this world happens to fail. The inevitable result is that the religious dimension of our lives will be sadly neglected and, when we grow old, we will find that we have invested far too much in the worldly bank and now wonder whether there is still time to correct our mistake.

Fortunately for us, God is well aware of our human frailty and is willing to forgive our youthful foolishness, which may last till retirement or beyond, and to provide us with the opportunity to make up for the time lost.

It is in some ways like the inveterate smoker who, even if he quits smoking only late in life, can still derive most of the benefits from that courageous decision. The one thing we want to avoid at all cost is having people say of us: "Sadly, older but no wiser!"

And so Paul proudly proclaims "Christ crucified." How we strive, over and over again, to separate him from the cross! But Christ has no meaning without his unconditional love and such love leads inevitably to self-sacrifice...and the ultimate sign of such self-giving is his crucifixion. This is "a stumbling block to Jews," in the sense that, at that time, many of them were placing such a high premium on "good deeds" and could not understand therefore that the most significant good deed is to accept the suffering that comes from loving and trusting.

Christ crucified is also "foolishness to Gentiles." The Gentiles that Paul knew were the same people whom he calls "Greeks," that is, those who were famous for their rational analysis. After all, they were heirs of Aristotle and Plato. When Paul spoke to them, at Athens, about the resurrection of the body, many laughed at him (Acts 17:32). They rightly extolled the virtues of intellectual life but they wrongly placed this kind of life above the gift of unselfish love.

Jesus worked spectacular miracles in Galilee and he argued mightily with the Scribes and Pharisees but he was never more powerful or more brilliant than when he died on the cross out of love for us. Few things seem more foolish and unpromising than loving others indiscriminately. Yet this kind of love is far more powerful that the greatest feats of intellectual or physical strength. It is in that sense that "God's foolishness" of unselfish love "is wiser than human wisdom," and "God's weakness" of service to others "is stronger than human strength."

These words are profoundly consoling to those of us whose minds and arms are showing the frailty of old age. For we can love now better than ever and we should see this as the wonderful opportunity that we have been waiting for.

6

CALLED TO BE WITH CHRIST IN GLORY

So if you have been raised with Christ, seek the things that are above, where Christ is, seated at the right hand of God. Set your minds on things that are above, not on things that are on earth, for you have died, and your life is hidden with Christ in God. When Christ who is your life is revealed, then you also will be revealed with him in glory (Col 3:1-4).

It is perfectly natural that we should be immersed in the affairs of this world because, after all, this is where we live and eat and love and succeed and fail. It is not healthy to be so negative about this world that one is tempted to live in some illusion about an ideal existence or, worse still, in some alcohol or drug induced denial of reality. God made the world and called it "very good" (Gen 1:31). Therefore, we too should try to see and appreciate its goodness and beauty.

At the same time, as Paul reminds us in this text, we need to recognize the definite limitations of this world. It is a passing reality and our sojourn in it is also severely limited. During the relatively short days of youth we can perhaps ignore this reality, but its truth will gradually impose itself on our con-sciousness…and ever more insistently as the years pass by. We don't expect children to be thinking about death, but by the same token it is not wise for older persons to be ignoring death.

This represents a tragic scenario for those who have never discovered the gospel and have not heard or heeded the promise of eternal life that God has given us in that gospel. But for us favored ones, the situation is totally different. This means that, as Paul says, we "must seek the things that are above, where Christ is seated, at the right hand of God." In other words, we must gradually but persistently come to the awareness that our real life is not to be found in this world at all. This is at most a kind of staging area for the journey that takes us to the place that a loving creator has reserved for us.

This mental transition from earth to heaven may seem to be very difficult or even impossible. However, most of us have made similar transitions before in our lives. I recall how dif-ficult it was for me, at the age of twelve, to leave my close-knit family on an isolated farm in order to attend a boarding high school many miles away. My body went there but my heart and my mind were still back at the farm. I used to try to imag-ine what my dad and mother as well as my twin brother and others would be doing at certain times of the day. That was still the real world for me.

Gradually, however, I adjusted to my new life and began to focus more and more on the classes and recreation and spiritual events of my new environment. Now that I have spent fifty plus years as a monk in the monastery that oper-ated that high school it is more familiar than that childhood world that I left long ago. The analogy is not perfect, but it does remind us that transitions are an essential part of our human experience.

We are assisted somewhat in making this transition when we go through the painful experience of losing good friends with whom we have spent most of our lives. I can still hear my Dad saying occasionally, as he read the daily obituaries, "There goes another good friend." But in some way this is how God ever so gently weans us away from this life and prepares us for the next. It is not a tragedy that we gradually begin to feel like strangers in this world, filled as it is with young people who don't remember our history.

If we really understand what is happening, we will follow Paul's advice and begin to set our minds "on things that are above." We will do this because we will finally understand that in baptism we "have died," and our lives are henceforth "hidden with Christ in God." We have died to self-centeredness to the extent that we have invested our lives in others, including those old (and sometimes very young) friends who have gone before us. And to the extent that we have become more conscious of others we have also acquired a new kind of life with Christ that makes us smile and rejoice in even difficult circumstances.

Paul ends with a glorious promise: "When Christ who is your life is revealed, then you also will be revealed with him in glory." What a joy that will be, to be caught up in the radiance of Christ's victory in a wonderful homeland where we belong in a way we have never known and from which we will never have to move again.

7

THE LORD IS OUR
FAITHFUL SHEPHERD

The LORD is my shepherd, I shall not want. He makes me lie down in green pastures; he leads me beside still waters; he restores my soul (Ps 23:1-3a).

It is unfortunate that most of us have little or no knowledge of the ancient and refined art of sheep herding. The Bible draws so much of its imagery from this art that I used to tell my students that we should have a flock of sheep on the lawn outside our classroom so that we might see how sheep behave and how they relate to their shepherd. This would be especially helpful in understanding this famous text about God as the shepherd of Israel.

The bond between sheep and shepherd is very strong and the sheep rely completely on the shepherd's commands. In the Near East, where rainfall is scarce and pasture is difficult to find, it is the knowledge and experience of the shepherd that makes the difference between life and death for the sheep in his care.

The shepherd must, first of all, know the territory well enough to be able to lead his flock to those narrow valleys where there will still be some fresh grass. Moreover, he must know where there are wells or watering holes during the long summer months when there is no rain at all. Having been a farm boy in western Pennsylvania, it always amazed me during my student days in Jerusalem that animals could survive without rain from May till October. And when it finally did rain, the drops of rain would at first be muddy as they cleansed the atmosphere!

The psalmist sees immediately the similarity between the relationship of sheep to shepherd and that of us believers to our loving God. In many circumstances of life, we must rely on the wisdom and strength of others. This is never more true than when we turn to the wisest and strongest of all—that One who gave us our lives and who knows how to lead us to places of nourishment and safety. It is for that reason that the psalmist can say, "Even though I walk through the darkest valley, I fear no evil; for you are with me; your rod and your staff—they comfort me" (Ps 23:4).

Jesus himself draws upon the imagery of sheep and shepherd when he calls himself the good shepherd: "I am the good shepherd. The good shepherd lays down his life for the sheep" (John 10:11). He contrasts this attitude of absolute devotion with that of the hired hand for whom tending the sheep is just a job and for whom the sheep are not worth the risk of one's life. The implication of this comparison could not be clearer. Jesus truly loves us and not only risks his life for us but gladly lays it down for our safety.

As we grow older, we become ever more aware of our dependence on others. It is most comforting, therefore, to know that the God who made us and who loves us is ready to care for all our needs, even at the cost of his own life. When

Jesus says that he is our good shepherd, he is guaranteeing that we can rely on his wisdom and love to take us through even the darkest valley to a broad, open land where we will find the ultimate nourishment and safety.

In our later years, we are far more likely to experience uncertainty and fear of the unknown. It is at such times that we need to hear the psalmist assure us that our loving God leads us "beside still waters." When that happens, the stillness of the meandering stream will calm our spirits. We will sense in particular the way that the water never ceases to come and is never afraid to continue on. God wants us too to "go with the flow" as we take life in stride and allow ourselves to be carried into the future with certain confidence that we will someday flow into the immense ocean that is God's love for us.

When we accept this rhythm of life, we will feel our confidence return to us. We will know then how the psalmist, and each of us, can say that God, the good shepherd, "restores my soul." When that happens, we will be able to breathe more deeply and to smile more readily. Most of all, we will be able to face the future with more courage and trust.

We should also be able to identify with the flock of the Good Shepherd when we notice that these sheep are almost totally dependent on the courage and wisdom of their leader. In ancient times, there were always wild animals following the flock, ready to pounce on any sheep that happened to wander away from the shepherd's care. We too can easily forget our own Good Shepherd and take chances that can be fatal. This is a reminder to pay attention to the Lord through fervent prayer.

8

STORING UP TREASURES IN HEAVEN

Do not store up for yourselves treasures on earth, where moth and rust consume and where thieves break in and steal; but store up for yourselves treasures in heaven, where neither moth nor rust consumes and where thieves do not break in and steal. For where your treasure is, there your heart will be also (Matt 6:19-21).

We always feel more secure when we possess something that can serve as a hedge against a rainy day. When I was a student in Jerusalem, I noticed how many Arab women had coins sewn into the scarves they wore on their heads. I was told that this was a safeguard against future times of hardship so that they would be protected from the misery of abject poverty and helplessness.

There is certainly nothing wrong with laying aside some small treasure for the future. But this sort of prudence can easily get out of hand. This happens when we begin to hoard resources to the extent that we become obsessed with how to increase our treasure and how to protect it. The gospel of Matthew recognizes this problem and warns us to keep our eyes on a very different kind of treasure.

In the days of Israel, the treasure being hoarded was usually clothing or grain, and the threat to such simple supplies was moth and rust. Rust is a fungus that attacks stored grain and makes it unfit for human consumption. The thieves were those who found it easier to plunder other people's property than to work hard for their own.

Today the treasure that encumbers us is more likely to be stocks or bonds or gold coins or a stamp or coin collection. We have all learned in recent years how volatile the stock market can be. And what good is a coin or stamp collection that is hidden away in a bank vault so that we cannot see it or even talk about it. But worst of all is the anxiety that comes from managing one's wealth. I once visited a wealthy family on the East Coast and, while I was soaking up the sun and enjoying the ocean waves, the father of this family was in the house checking out his investments! But the ultimate threat to one's precious worldly wealth is simply that you cannot take it with you.

We almost feel sorry for that wealthy farmer in Luke's gospel who had such a bountiful harvest that he was planning to build bigger barns for storing his bumper crops. In fact, he congratulated himself with the soliloquy: "Soul, you have ample goods laid up for many years; relax, eat, drink, be merry." But everything came crashing down around him when he heard God say, "You fool! This very night your life is being demanded of you. And the things you have prepared, whose will they be?" Luke then draws the same conclusion as Matthew when he says, "So it is with those who store up treasures for themselves but are not rich toward God" (Luke 12:19-21).

It is, of course, only prudent to make preparations for the uncertain future. But no one can gainsay the wisdom offered by the gospels, namely, that it is far more important to store up treasures in heaven. Such secure treasures are good deeds and loving service. At a certain critical point in life, we must make a fateful decision about whether we will devote most of our attention to self-preservation and self-concern or whether we will invest more and more of our time and talents in the lives of others. We can do this by volunteering, by generous support of agencies that help the poor or, where that is not possible, by being a friendly, supportive person in whatever situation we may find ourselves.

Older persons may not have much strength, and they may lack surplus material resources, but their touch is just as tender, or more so, than that of a twenty-year-old. And there are so many ways in which the wisdom and experience of older persons can be shared with others who are struggling to find their way. Then there is quiet, earnest and frequent prayer, which can accomplish so much more than anyone could imagine. The gospel is surely right when it tells us, "Where your treasure is, there your heart will be also." We will be blest indeed if we discover that our treasure is in God's keeping and that no one can ever take it away from us.

When we pray, we go to our true treasure house and, instead of counting gold coins, we count our blessings. As we do so we keep discovering more and more blessings that we had not noticed. And we keep feeling more and more grateful for the love of God in our lives. In this way, we are able to fill our minds with so much goodness that there is no longer any room for negative and depressing thoughts. A happy state indeed!

9

FINDING OUR TRUE HOME WITH JESUS

The next day John again was standing with two of his disciples, and as he watched Jesus walk by, he exclaimed, "Look, here is the Lamb of God!" The two disciples heard him say this, and they followed Jesus. When Jesus turned and saw them following, he said to them, "What are you looking for?" They said to him, "Rabbi, (which translated means Teacher), where are you staying?" He said to them, "Come and see." They came and saw where he was staying, and they remained with him that day. It was about four o'clock in the afternoon (John 1:35-39).

When John the Baptist pointed toward Jesus and declared him to be the "Lamb of God," he was making a messianic statement about the savior who was to come and who would offer himself for our salvation. The Baptist no doubt has in mind the prophecy of Isaiah where we read, "But he was wounded for our transgressions, crushed for our iniquities.... He was oppressed, and he was afflicted, yet he did not open his mouth; like a lamb that is led to the slaughter...so he did not open his mouth" (53:5, 7).

The two disciples of the Baptist, when they heard his surprising announcement, recognized its import and left him to follow Jesus. This prompted a rather strange exchange between Jesus and these two disciples. First of all, Jesus notices that they have joined him and says to them, "What are you looking for?" On one level, this is a simple question about their intentions. But, at a deeper, symbolic level, Jesus is recognizing in them one of the most basic characteristics of us human beings, namely, that we are forever looking for the meaning of life. We are, quite simply, endlessly searching beings, always looking for a Holy Grail or a Shangri La.

The response of the disciples also has a deeper meaning. They are not just asking where he resides. The Greek verb that is translated "staying" is also found in John's gospel in all those profound texts about the union of Jesus with his Father and with us. It these cases, it is translated "abide." For example, Jesus tells us, "Abide in me as I abide in you" (15:4). With this in mind, we can understand the question of the disciples as, "Where do we belong?" or, "Where is our true home?" In other words, they are asking the question that we humans have been wondering about ever since the beginning: Where do we really belong and can we find peace?

Suddenly the answer of Jesus to their question takes on a very special importance. He does not tell them that they belong in heaven, although that would also be true (as many of us learned from the Baltimore catechism). Rather, he tells them that they can only find their true home by walking with him as they embrace his wisdom in their daily experience. Once again, therefore, John is insisting that the real meaning of our lives will be revealed only in our personal experience of the presence and love of God in this world. It is nothing less than an invitation to that mystical experience that enables us to see how the whole world becomes transparent, as it were, to reveal the reality of God's loving presence in every circumstance of life.

The evangelist tells us then that "They remained with him that day. It was about four o'clock in the afternoon." Although this statement sounds like a very obvious historical detail, I am convinced that it has a deeper meaning also. First of all, a "day" in the Bible can easily stand for a period of special opportunity and could mean that the disciples spent the most important years of their lives with him. But what about the specific time of "four o'clock in the afternoon?" It is very tempting to see here a reference to that "time of the evening breeze" when God walked in the garden of Eden looking for Adam and Eve (Genesis 3:8)!

In Genesis the man and woman were hiding from God. Now, at long last, they are looking for the meaning of life from the one, whom they call "Rabbi," that is, "Teacher." Adam and Eve had looked for the meaning of life in a choice that brought tragedy to them. The situation is reversed now and, at long last, we descendants of those first parents, are looking for the meaning of life in the only place where it can ever be found, that is, in the company of Jesus.

Many of us older folks have had very busy lives and we have not spent as much time as we should have in walking with the Master as students who are eager to learn. But it is not too late to learn from him who is "gentle and humble in heart" (Matthew 11:29). He will be ever so patient with us as he guides us to our true home. We will walk with the Lord by making room in our minds and hearts for him and especially when we pray for a share of his wisdom. There is absolutely no better or more profitable way to spend our time.

10

REJOICING IN THE LORD

Rejoice in the LORD always; again I will say, Rejoice. Let your gentleness be known to everyone. The Lord is near. Do not worry about anything, but in everything by prayer and supplication with thanksgiving let your requests be made known to God. And the peace of God, which surpasses all understanding, will guard your hearts and your minds in Christ Jesus (Phil 4:4-7).

When Paul says that we should "rejoice in the Lord," he is not just making a suggestion; he is issuing a command. And he is so insistent on this point that he repeats his order. We need to take these words of Paul seriously because we know how many hardships he faced and how many good reasons he had for not rejoicing. I'm sure that Paul would say, Yes, I have endured many trials but please note that I said, "Rejoice in the Lord." The source of my rejoicing is not some accomplishment of mine but something wonderful that the Lord has done in me.

What God has done in both Paul and ourselves is to have given us the gift of faith which enables us to see the hidden goodness of God's presence and love in a world that is filled with much darkness. Blessed John XXIII said to a group of seminarians near the end of his life: "Every day is a good day—a good day for living—and a good day for dying." I take this to mean that this holy man, during his long lifetime, had become so accustomed, through the power of his faith, to call each day "a good day" that, when that final "dark" day approached, he discovered that he was able, indeed impelled, to call it also a "good day."

When we allow our faith to reveal the goodness in life, in spite of everything, we become "gentle" persons, that is, we see the futility of anger or fear or worry as we rest securely in the arms of our loving God. And then we can say with Paul, not "The end is near," but "The Lord is near!" We are told that some who die actually have their eyes focused on some distant horizon as if they can see beyond the end and are ready to greet the Lord who is now nearer than ever before in their lives.

Whether we are granted that grace or not, we can follow the advice of Paul not to worry about anything. For we already know that God's arms are stretched out toward us, ready to embrace us and to welcome us into a homeland of peace and joy. In the meantime, we fill the time of our waiting, as Paul says, with "prayer and supplication with thanksgiving." Such prayer and thanksgiving may very well be without words. But if we want to use words, the ancient "Jesus prayer" would be a good choice: "Lord Jesus Christ, Son of God, have mercy on me a sinner."

I have found it helpful to say the first part of this Jesus prayer as I breathe in, as if filling myself with the power of Jesus, Son of God. The second half of the prayer is said then as

I exhale, as if ridding myself of the sinfulness that still exists in me. When this is done very slowly and deliberately, it brings peace and harmony as it drives out fear and panic. This is not some magical or mechanical trick but simply a useful way to become more aware of the presence of God, which is more real and more important than anything else we can imagine.

Paul says that our prayer must also include thanksgiving. A very wise person told me once that the primary sign of a true Christian is that he or she has become a profoundly grateful person. A classic example of this is St. Thérèse, the Little Flower. In her last days, when she was wracked with pain and filled with doubts about the goodness of God, she was able to say that, when she looked back over her whole life, she could only exclaim, "Everything is gift!" She surely was not lying when she gave this testimony. But she could see that the goodness of God in her life was so much more important than anything else could possibly be.

Finally, Paul tells us that such a victory of faith and prayer in our lives will bring about a wonderful experience of peace and serenity. This is not the shallow peace that we can discover on our own, but the peace that only God can give. That is why Paul says that it "surpasses all understanding." When we grow older, we can easily be beset by all kinds of confusion and anxiety as we try to deal with limitations that we have never known before. If we ask God, he will surely "guard our hearts and minds in Christ Jesus." Such protection and peace will be so much more helpful than any benefit we may seek from drugs or medications. We will truly be resting in the hand of God.

11

THE LORD IS OUR FORTRESS

I love you, O LORD, my strength. The LORD is my rock, my fortress, and my deliverer, my God, my rock in whom I take refuge, my shield, and the horn of my salvation, my stronghold (Ps 18:1-2).

There are times when we feel young and strong. We have so much energy that it can be squandered in seemingly aimless play. I can recall the days when I would teach all morning and then, in the early afternoon, head for the volleyball court for several fast games with our seminary students. On the way, I would leap high in the corridor to see if I could touch the ceiling. In those carefree days of youthful energy, there was no sense of the heaviness and cautious ways of my present older days.

In these latter days, one can feel the limits of one's energy and a consequent necessary caution about taking on taxing projects. Energy must be carefully conserved and, even with all that prudence, one often feels inadequate to the task undertaken. Sometimes, the voice sounds thin and breathing can require a conscious effort.

It may be sufficient at such times to wait a while until one feels stronger again. But it soon becomes clear that simply waiting for a better moment is not always very successful. In such circumstances, we really need to look outside ourselves for a source of energy and confidence that we can no longer expect to find in our own bodies and psyches.

These words from Psalm 18 are a wonderful basis for such a renewed confidence. The metaphors are powerful: God is my "rock"—a solid foundation on which I can stand with a deep sense of security. He is my "fortress"—a place of refuge behind thick, high walls that are able to withstand every assault of fear, anxiety or depression.

God is also my "deliverer"—that strong one who can reach down and pluck me out of the deep, turbulent waters that threaten to engulf me. An inexperienced swimmer who panics never forgets the one who pulls him to safety. God is also my "shield"—the armor that protects me from the powerful strokes of my adversary. He is the "horn of my salvation"— an image taken from the horn of the ox which is a projection of that powerful neck that, once set, can never be turned aside. God is equally determined to lead us to salvation and glory…if we love him and trust his mercy.

All of these very concrete and vivid images come together to declare the consistent love of God who is always ready to defend us and rescue us no matter how desperate our situation may be. This does not mean that we will be cured of every illness or rescued from every bout of depression. But it does tell us that we are not alone in the struggle.

Moreover, we are told to be confident that our loving Lord will rescue us in the end. Illness or weakness or fear must be recognized, not as the final victory of darkness, but rather as the struggle that leads to a new birth and a much better kind of life. The God who is our rock of refuge leads us to ultimate victory over all the dark powers that confront us.

It is true, of course, that the maxim, "easier said than done," applies here perhaps more than anywhere else. Nonetheless, it has been my experience that we need to repeat these words of the psalmist, over and over again, until we are able to hear them and feel their power. There have been many times when I have said these words in choir when I was struggling with a bad cold or felt burdened by cares and responsibilities. There was no magical cure, of course, but I did feel the healing power in these divine words.

The secret is to say these prayers often and with as much faith as we can muster. Such faith enables us to trust the power of God's words and allows these words to enter our prison and break open the doors for us. This is especially true when we say the Lord's Prayer. We call God our loving Father even when we do not feel the love and care that is implied in that name. Nonetheless, as we repeat this prayer and address God as Father, we will gradually find that our experience in a sense "catches up to our words," and we begin to discover the love that has always been there and which we now feel and enjoy in a whole new way.

Repeating words that express how we ought to feel, even if that is not our present experience, can also have the great advantage of filling our minds with healthy words and thoughts and thereby preventing dangerous and toxic thoughts from taking a foothold there. We can't always keep such thoughts from entering our minds but we can replace them with good thoughts once we recognize their threat to us.

12

DISCOVERING THE GIFT OF GOD

For there is no distinction, since all have sinned and fall short of the glory of God; they are now justified by his grace as a gift, through the redemption that is in Christ Jesus, whom God put forward as a sacrifice of atonement by his blood, effective through faith (Rom 3:22b-25).

In the first chapters of his Letter to the Romans, St. Paul is deeply concerned about the desperate situation of sin-burdened humanity. When he says, "there is no distinction," he is referring to his previous argument that not only the Gentiles are sinners but that his fellow Jews also are in need of liberation from the bondage of sin, since they have compromised their privilege of revelation by refusing to observe its precepts.

In one of the most important statements of the New Testament, St. Paul then declares his conviction that there is only one way to escape from the crushing weight of sin and that is through the gift of faith. Nowhere in the Bible is faith defined. It is far too personal and mysterious for that. But St. Paul gives us a clear sense of the nature of this divine gift in this passage from Romans.

He tells us that the effect of faith is to be "justified," that is, to be made right with God, to be restored to God's friendship. The critical words are: "by his grace, as a gift." A more literal translation would be "by his favor or kindness," and "after the manner of a gift." We note that St. Paul is being redundant here so as to emphasize the fact that the gift of faith is intended to make us aware of the gift of God in our lives. In a word, it is a gift that opens us to seeing the goodness, often hidden, that is everywhere in our world.

When I was a student in the seminary, we memorized a definition of faith that was true but very incomplete. We learned that faith is "an assent of the intellect to the truths of Revelation." But it is so much more than that. It touches every fiber of our being, not just our intellect. It gives us the ability to see that, underneath the surface of evil and violence in life, there is a mighty river of God's goodness. Without the divinely provided insight of faith, we are condemned to see only the surface where there is mostly sin and violence. Faith enables us to penetrate beneath that surface to a great reservoir of goodness, which God has placed in life and which he wants us to discover.

This sea of goodness is made available to us through the "redemption," that is, the saving sacrifice of Jesus. It is concentrated in his person, from which it emanates to illuminate and beautify all of reality. St. Paul goes on to tell us that God the Father put Jesus forward "as a sacrifice of atonement." In other words, the loving self-sacrifice of Jesus became the event that "soaked up," as it were, the indignation of God in the presence of our sinfulness. Henceforth, we need only to draw close to Jesus, and to make his loving concern part of our own way of living, in order to participate in the inexhaustible source of forgiveness that is now available to us.

The gift of faith thus enables us to be firmly convinced of the ultimate victory of goodness over evil, not only now but also in the future. This is reflected in a beautiful text from the First Letter of John: "And this is the victory that conquers the world, our faith" (5:4). In other words, the darkness and negativity of the world, dominated by sin and despair, are cancelled by the much more powerful presence of goodness and hope revealed to us by our faith. We want to think that this is so, and faith gives us the firm conviction of this truth.

Although this vision of faith makes all the difference in any period of our lives, it becomes much more significant in our later years. Our growing uncertainty about the future and our more fragile situation can easily become a breeding-ground for doubt and hopelessness. That is when our faith comes into its own and supplies that firm conviction about the superior power of God's love and goodness, no matter what our plight may be. This is so true that we must legitimately wonder whether we can possibly know what faith means prior to age sixty-five! For it is only in these later years that our joyful expectation must be based on something other than our own strength and determination.

To be an optimistic and confident older person does not depend then upon our will-power or our acting ability; it is the natural and inevitable result of a living and active faith. Surely there is no more beautiful witness to the presence and power of Jesus in our lives than the smiling, radiant faces of those who are filled with faith and who are living proof of the victory of this faith over the hopelessness of the world.

13

TRUSTING OUR ANGELS

But (Tobias') mother began to weep, and said to Tobit, "Why is it that you have sent my child away? Is he not the staff of our hand as he goes in and out before us?.... Tobit said to her, "Do not worry; our child will leave in good health and return to us in good health. Your eyes will see him on the day when he returns to you in good health.... For a good angel will accompany him; his journey will be successful, and he will come back in good health." So she stopped weeping (Tobit 5:18, 21-22; 6:1).

There is something very poignant about the weeping of Tobias' mother. She trusts her husband, Tobit, and she knows that it is time for her son to take responsibility for the future of their family, but it is so hard to see him set out on a long journey to an unknown land. Her husband has been a very observant Jew (almost to a fault), but that has not prevented him from being blinded by the fresh droppings of a sparrow. If God could not protect him for such a fortuitous (and embarrassing) accident, how can she be sure that he will protect her only son, the "staff" on whom they hope to rely in their old age?

Tobit must have had his misgivings also, but he has trusted in God for so long that it is too late to look elsewhere for help. In the Book of Tobit he stands for the people of Israel, who have been living for a long time under foreign domination and are trying desperately to keep their faith in God alive. In a very real sense, the weeping mother and the trusting father are two aspects of an Israel that struggles to remain faithful to the God of Exodus while wondering every day why this God has not noticed their terrible plight.

When Tobit tells his wife that she should not worry, one must wonder whether he says this from his human heart or from the wellspring of his faith. His firm declaration that "our child will leave in good health and return to us in good health" is just another way of saying that God is in his heaven and all is right with the world. There is no immediate evidence for this but it is a case of faith conquering history. This victory is in the future but it is certain nonetheless. We recall the words of 1 John: "And this is the victory that conquers the world, our faith" (5:4). In this case, as in the plight of Tobit, the "world" is a code word for all the dangers and threats in life. Only faith in God's goodness has the power to overcome what seems at times insuperable.

The phrase, "in good health," recurs like a refrain in this story. Tobias will leave in good health and return in the same good health. This is not just a reference to his physical well being. He will come back from his long journey and will also bring with him the cure for his father's blindness. Everything will make sense in the end. In the meantime, hardly anything makes sense. This is frequently the experience of Israel in her history and it is the experience of us too as we grow older and begin to feel the limits of our strength and the need to let go of so many plans.

How is it possible to live in peace and hope under such circumstances? We hear the answer in the comforting words of Tobit to his wife: "For a good angel will accompany him; his journey will be successful, and he will come back in good health." We know from the story that this good angel is Raphael and it is clear that this angel, like all the others, is in fact an extension of God's love and care into every situation in our lives. Angels are representatives of God's goodness in a world where chaos often seems to be in control.

It is not as if God sends an angel to deal with problems in the world and then turns his attention to other matters. The angels are, quite simply, the proof of God's concern for us. But the angels can come only when we believe in God's goodness and ask for his help. Abraham didn't summon the three angels when he and Sarah were old and forlorn at Mamre. He believed in the promise of God, and God's response was to send the angels. This was God's way of being present to one who had never wavered in his faith and trust.

As we grow older and life becomes ever more mysterious, it is important to remember that faith does not grow stronger in the easy days when life makes sense. It is a gift that grows with the challenges that we meet. And when it becomes like our second nature, we will know that God has sent his angel to accompany us and to make us come home "in good health." Then, like Tobias' mother, we too will be able to stop weeping.

14

LET US LOVE ONE ANOTHER

I give you a new commandment, that you love one another. Just as I have loved you, you also should love one another. By this everyone will know that you are my disciples, if you have love for one another (John 13:34-35).

These words of Jesus appear in John's gospel at the beginning of his "farewell discourse," which precedes the story of his passion and death. One of the primary elements of such a farewell discourse is the advice given by the patriarch or matriarch who is saying Goodbye to his or her children and grandchildren. Such advice is especially important because it summarizes all the advice that has been given in the course of a long life.

In the case of Jesus also, the disciples have heard many words of wisdom but now he selects from all of them this most important and truly indispensable word of advice: "I give you a new commandment, that you love one another." It is called a "new" commandment because it surpasses all the many precepts that have preceded and which have been concerned mainly with external behavior. Although external behavior will always be important, it has value only if it results from the primary commandment to love one another. When such behavior is based on love, it does not demand gratitude in return and does not lead to pride and self-satisfaction.

Jesus is aware that "love" can mean almost anything—from selfish infatuation to genuine self-giving for the sake of others. Accordingly, he adds immediately, "Just as I have loved you, you also should love one another." Jesus himself becomes the model of what authentic love really means. He did not make himself the center of attention and service, but spent himself for the good of others, even to the ultimate gift of his own life. He could have fled from the garden of Gethsemane with the disciples, but he knew that his heavenly Father had a mission of self-sacrifice for him and he was faithful to that calling to the very end.

It is also true, however, that Jesus does more than offer us a perfect model of what true love means. He knows that we could never love as he does by our own resources. And so this commandment carries with it a promise to provide for us the gift that will enable us to be loving and caring persons in spite of our human frailty. In fact, this gift of God is so powerful that it can enable us at times to be nothing less than heroic in our concern and care for others. With the command, therefore, comes also the help we need in order to achieve this ideal.

As we grow older, it may be difficult or impossible to attend church or to be helpful to others in the way that we would like. But the words of Jesus remind us that the really important thing is that we love others in the ways that are possible. That will often mean just a smile or a pleasant and positive comment. It may mean saying our prayers at home if the weather is bad and we cannot go out. The important thing is that we trust the Lord and try to realize that being a blessing in the lives of others is worth more than all the activity that we may previously have been accustomed to.

Jesus continues with a statement that deserves our closest attention: "By this everyone will know that you are my disciples, if you have love for one another." In other words, Jesus himself is telling us that the primary and indispensable characteristic of a faithful follower of him is to be a loving, sensitive and positive person in all the circumstances of life. Our identity as Christians, therefore, does not depend primarily on what prayers we say or what liturgy we use or what membership card we may carry in our purse or wallet! These things are not unimportant, but they are completely secondary to the one essential characteristic of true Christians, namely, that they love one another.

We are almost afraid to think about the implications of this solemn statement by Jesus. When we think of all the wars that have been fought by Christians, and of how much distrust and discord still exist between the various churches that call themselves Christian, we really need to examine our consciences and acknowledge how far we still are from the ideal that Jesus taught. I spent two years as a student in Jerusalem and it was really discouraging to see how much distrust existed between the various Christian groups that used the Church of the Holy Sepulchre. Even the guardians of this most holy shrine could not bear effective witness to the all-embracing love of Jesus. Age is supposed to give us some wisdom and, if that is true, we surely need to testify to the whole world that we honor the words of Jesus as we try more and more to be a loving presence in our world.

15

EXPELLING DEMONS FROM OUR LIVES

And (Jesus) cured many who were sick with various diseases, and cast out many demons.... And he went throughout Galilee, proclaiming the message in their synagogues and casting out demons (Mark 1:34, 39).

The gospels of Matthew, Mark and Luke make frequent references to the ministry of Jesus in Galilee. It is not too difficult to understand Jesus' ministry of healing or to recognize his power over the forces of nature. But it is somewhat surprising to note how often we are told that Jesus drove out demons. We need to look closely at this activity of Jesus so that we may see the deeper implications of what he did and how this might be understood in a modern situation.

It is clear that the healing ministry of Jesus was intended to draw attention to himself and to provide divine credentials that would support his message of salvation. It should be obvious that Jesus did not perform these miracles simply to show that he was a compassionate person. After all, those who were cured got sick later and died anyway. And those whom he raised from the dead also died eventually...for the second time! Besides, we can scarcely maintain that he ceased to be compassionate when he no longer worked miracles.

In order to understand the deeper implications of Jesus' activity in Galilee, we need to see the connection with his baptism, which propelled him toward this unique ministry. In Jesus' baptism, the appearance of the Spirit over him in the form of a dove was a clear symbolic sign that a new creation was about to take place, since the bird or dove is inseparable from the original creation in Genesis as well as from the new creation after the flood.

The activity of Jesus in Galilee is, therefore, an illustration of the nature of this new world. It will involve an influx of divine love, concentrated in the person of Jesus, but also flowing through him with such power as to be able potentially to transform everything. In Galilee, Jesus shows us the nature of this new creation by reaching out to all who are in bondage and by liberating them, at least temporarily. The ultimate liberation from bondage will come only through his death and resurrection, but it is important to show the purpose of his mission in graphic and understandable terms at the beginning of his ministry. In fact, Jesus seems to have been drawn especially to the paralytics, for they represented human bondage in an especially dramatic way.

It is from this perspective also that we need to see the meaning of the frequent interventions of Jesus to liberate those possessed by demons. We must be careful not to be overly influenced by lurid stories of demon possession, such as we see in novels or movies. In the ancient world, the one constant characteristic of demon possession was a power that caused the victim to be disorganized or contorted, either physically or psychologically. Physically, this would mean loss of control over one's body; psychically, it would mean loss of one's center of identity with a consequent sense of abandonment and despair.

In terms of the biblical notion of the universe, the demons would be agents of the original chaos that preceded creation. The ancient Hebrews always thought that the forces of chaos were trying to "take back" the created world that had come into being through God's goodness. Since Jesus came to renew and fulfill creation, it was inevitable that he should be challenged by these agents of the original chaos, and it was imperative that he should show his power over them.

If there are demons today that we should be concerned about, they are not the poltergeists or denizens of haunted houses. These are mild compared to the real demons, who are far more likely to be those mysterious forces that destroy the peace and harmony that we need for happy living. Moreover, these "demonic" powers seem to be felt especially in our later years. This may be due in part to the fact that we have more time to wonder about such things, but it is also because we are particularly vulnerable to fear and anxiety as we grow older.

It seems that such turbulent thoughts and feelings are more likely to take hold of us when we feel alone or too weak to do what we used to do. At such times, all the negative powers in life seem far more fearsome than at other times. This also suggests how we can best resist their influence, for Jesus is always present and concerned for us, and when we call this to mind we can scatter those dark forces, just as he did in the hills of Galilee.

16

HAVING THE POSITIVE SPIRIT OF DAVID

(King Saul) waited seven days, the time appointed by Samuel; but Samuel did not come to Gilgal, and the people began to slip away from Saul. So Saul said, "Bring the burnt offering here to me.... And he offered the burnt offering. As soon as he had finished offering the burnt offering, Samuel arrived.... Samuel said, "What have you done?" Saul replied, "When I saw that the people were slipping away from me, and that you did not come within the days appointed...I forced myself, and offered the burnt offering." Samuel said to Saul, "You have done foolishly...now your kingdom will not continue" (1Sam 13:8-14).

Saul was Israel's first king and his early victories over the Philistines made the people think that he had been an ideal choice. But there was a fatal flaw in King Saul, which became apparent when he faced the challenge of the failure of the prophet Samuel to arrive in time to offer sacrifice in preparation for a difficult battle. It seems very hard to fault Saul for his action, done with the best of intentions, since he waited seven full days and acted only in desperation. Nonetheless, Samuel tells him that God found him wanting and that his days as king were at an end.

Not only does Samuel tell Saul that God has rejected him as king of Israel, but he also rubs salt in the wound by announcing the selection of a new king in his place: "The LORD has sought out a man after his own heart; and the LORD has appointed him to be ruler over his people" (1 Sam 13:14). The new king will be David, Israel's greatest king and a model of the Messiah. Years later, Jesus himself seems quite happy to be known as "son of David."

It is important to note that both Saul and David, though undoubtedly historical kings of Israel, are presented in the Bible also as symbolic figures who model for us two different ways of relating to God and to life. Saul is the tragic king, who could never seem to please God and who died by his own hand. By contrast, David is the blessed king who, in spite of sinfulness, remained always in touch with God and became the model of a successful human being. No doubt the Bible exaggerates this contrast so that we do not miss the point.

It is of paramount importance that we discover the nature of the flaw in Saul's relationship to God so that we can be sure to avoid that in our own lives. After all, it cannot be a simple matter of public sinfulness, for Saul's sin was scarcely more than a peccadillo, whereas David committed a truly mortal sin when he had Uriah killed in order to cover up his affair with Bathsheba. Rather, it is a question of the contrasting nature of their belief in God. They both believed in God and in the goodness of God, but that is the easy part. Saul could not believe in the goodness of God's world and, above all, he could not believe in the goodness of Saul!

As a consequence, Saul was always afraid of making a mistake. He could not trust his instincts, and lost one opportunity after another, because he was never ready to seize the moment. David was just the opposite. He had such a positive attitude toward life that he not only took his share of it but sometimes reached into God's territory. But because he trusted the goodness of God, he was also able to believe that God would forgive him. So he took his punishment and came out looking better than ever.

It is interesting to imagine how David would have handled the situation in which Samuel scolded Saul and said that God would take the kingdom away from him. I think that David would have waited perhaps a day and then would have offered the sacrifice. When Samuel challenged him, he would have answered, "You were late, and if it happens one more time you are no longer my chaplain!" And Samuel would have said, "Thank God, we have a real king in Israel!"

I think we have the spirit of both David and Saul in us. Saul tells us to be very cautious and to look for all that might go wrong in life; he is fearful, anxious and negative. David tells us to trust life and to be positive and hopeful in all circumstances. Needless to say, Saul's voice in us becomes stronger as we grow older. But it is terribly important that we listen to David, whose voice is reinforced in the witness of Jesus, son of David.

The Saul of the New Testament is Judas, who could not trust the message of Jesus when things didn't go the way he had planned. He wanted a political Messiah who at most could offer a perishable earthly kingdom, whereas Jesus had come as divine Savior with an eternal kingdom. Judas, like Saul, ended a suicide, because he could not trust God's goodness. He simply could not hope enough. We must not make the same mistake. The "David attitude" will see us through even the most difficult trials.

17

GOD'S MESSAGE COMES FROM THE HEART

No one has ever seen God. It is God the only Son, who is close to the Father's heart, who has made him known (John 1:18). One of his disciples—the one whom Jesus loved—was reclining next to him (John 13:23).

For John the Evangelist, the career of Jesus began, not at Bethlehem, but in the infinite reaches of eternity. He was the eternal Word of God long before he took on a human nature in the womb of the Virgin Mary and received the name "Jesus." The purpose of this incarnation of the eternal Word is expressed in the very name that John gives him, for he is the Word, that is, the revelation of the hidden God. And the essence of this revelation is that that hidden God is the loving Father of Jesus and, through him, of ourselves also.

God has always seemed distant to us human beings. Even Moses, to whom God spoke as to a friend, was not able to see His face (see Exodus 33:20). But all that changed when the divine Word took on our human nature and began to dwell with us. Having come from the bosom of this unseen God, he is able to reveal to us all his secrets. That is the meaning of the last verse of the Prologue to John's gospel, where we are told that Jesus, as divine Word, was "close to the Father's heart."

According to the literal meaning of the Greek text, the divine Word was "in the bosom of the Father," but the translation I have chosen captures precisely the deeper meaning of that phrase. For to be in the bosom of the Father means to be able to hear the heartbeat of the Father and thus to know all his secrets. These secrets concern the unconditional love that God has for all creation.

Jesus does far more, however, than simply tell us about the Father's love for us. He becomes in his person an extension of that love to us. This means that when he gives his life for us, he is showing us how much we are loved by the Father also. That is why he says to Philip, "Whoever has seen me has seen the Father" (John 14:9). In other words, the love that you see in me is the same love that exists in the Father.

That is also why Jesus can say, "As the Father has loved me, so I have loved you; abide in my love" (John 15:9). On the all too frequent days when we feel alone or forlorn or unloved, we should read these words, over and over again. Jesus becomes then the bond that links us to the all-powerful love of the Father. If we really understood this, we would glow with the light and warmth of that infinite goodness.

But we have another witness to this liberating truth about God's love for us. The author of the gospel of John is called, "the disciple whom Jesus loved," because he experienced the power of that love and now wishes to bear witness to it for our sake. We know this because of the position of the Beloved Disciple so near to Jesus at the Last Supper. In fact, he is said to have "reclined next to him." Regardless of what the exact arrangement of the places at the Last Supper may have been, the author of the gospel wants us to know that this Beloved Disciple is in a position to hear the heartbeat of Jesus, just as Jesus heard the heartbeat of his heavenly Father.

If this "chain" of witnesses is so direct and so powerful, we have to wonder why we are so often almost totally unaware of it. The answer cannot be that God has lost interest in us or that time has diluted in some way the power of God's love. The sad fact is that we are so distracted and so unfocused in our lives that we see and hear almost everything except what we need to see and hear and what God very much wants us to see and hear.

I am convinced that we need to set aside some quality time to listen to God speaking to us in the center of our being and telling us how much we are loved and how much we will miss if we do not make room for him in our lives. One of the nicest things we can do for our friends is to listen to them with all the attention that we can muster. It is no different with God, our best of friends. We need to say to God, "I am all ears; tell me what I need to know." And we can be certain that God will reveal to us, in a thousand quiet, gentle ways, what he revealed to Jesus at his baptism (and in our baptism too): "You are my beloved child; I love you more than you will ever know." In our later years, we usually have more time to listen in this way, and we surely need to hear God's comforting words more than ever before in our lives.

18

WALKING IN THE NEWNESS OF LIFE

Therefore we have been buried with (Christ) by baptism into death, so that, just as Christ was raised from the dead by the glory of the Father, so we too might walk in newness of life. For if we have been united with him in a death like his, we will certainly be united with him in a resurrection like his.... But if we have died with Christ, we believe that we will also live with him (Rom 6:4-5, 8).

Our Christian baptism probably occurred in our infancy, which means that we have no memory of it whatsoever. If someone had not told us or if we did not see our baptismal certificate, we would never know that it had happened. In fact, however, our baptism is a critically important event in our lives. This means that we must carefully examine what really happened long ago on that blessed day of our baptism, and above all we must carefully ponder what our sponsors promised in our names.

What they promised is that we declare ourselves dead to sinful selfishness and alive to the love that reaches out to help others in every way that we can and that they need. As soon as

we are old enough to understand the meaning of those promises, we must claim them in our own names and resolve to live
out all their implications. The fact that many adult Christians
are only vaguely aware of this obligation does not in any way
lessen the importance of such a discovery.

When Paul says that we are buried with Christ in baptism,
he is telling us that we have "died" to selfishness in all its
many manifestations and are now committed to live as Jesus
did in love and self-giving for the sake of others. To the degree
that this happens, we begin to "walk in newness of life." For
dying to sin means living for loving service, and that amounts
to being born again into a life like that of Jesus.

For our secular culture, this is a foolish thing to do. For it
means that we are renouncing that absolute quest for power
and control which secular culture considers the very hallmark
of success. There is nothing wrong with seeking power but
only on condition that this quest is for the purpose of loving
service. After all, God showed his immense power to the Pharaoh, but in the end it was his love that liberated the Hebrew
slaves because it gave them the courage to leave that place of
bondage.

Being united with Jesus will guarantee new life for us
because that is exactly what it did for him. He did not protect
his life from the demands of love and so he died very young.
But the same commitment to love that brought his early death
also produced his glorious resurrection. Paul wants us to see
the implications for our own lives. We have a strong urge to
protect ourselves from the needs of others but we must resist
that temptation because, if we succeed in insulating ourselves
from the demands of love, we will end up losing everything.
All the gospels tell us that the one who keeps his life in this

world, i.e. disregards the demands of love, will lose that life in the next world.

There is a considerable risk, of course, in allowing oneself to be in some sense consumed by the needs of others. That is why Paul wants us to look at Christ and to see in him that the outcome of loving others to the end is indeed a new and unending life that makes our present life seem like sleepwalking. To be "united with him in a death like his" means to commit oneself to loving concern for others, not necessarily in some heroic fashion, but nonetheless in a way that really cuts into our selfish tendencies.

What Paul has to say is of crucial importance for those of us who are getting on in years. Maybe we haven't been as unselfish as we should have been, since selfish tendencies are so subtle and persistent. It has been my experience that, when we bravely throw selfishness out the front door, we scarcely have the door closed until it is coming in the back door! Thus commitment to unselfishness requires constant vigilance and close examination of our motives.

But the reward for a truly unselfish and generous and thoughtful life is rich beyond words. Paul sums it up with admirable simplicity: "For if we have died with Christ, we believe that we will also live with him." And we cannot possibly imagine what a glorious life that will be. As Paul asserted elsewhere, "No eye had seen nor ear heard, nor the human heart conceived, what God has prepared for those who love him" (1 Cor 2:9). There are so many ways in which we older persons can be thoughtful and generous...and God cannot wait to show us the blessed consequences.

19

FAITH ENABLES US TO OVERCOME THE GIANTS OF FEAR AND DESPAIR

All the Israelites, when they saw (Goliath), fled from him and were very much afraid.... Saul said to David, "You are not able to go against this Philistine to fight with him; for you are just a boy, and he has been a warrior from his youth.... David put his hand in his bag, took out a stone, slung it, and struck the Philistine on his forehead; the stone sank into his fore-head, and he fell face down on the ground (1 Samuel 17:24, 33, 49).

We are all familiar with the story of David and Goliath. At least we know that Goliath was a giant and that David, a mere boy, had no chance to defeat him. For that reason, this story of David and Goliath represents the ultimate example of the victory of an underdog. The kernel of this story may very well be historical, but the Bible does not record it simply to tell us what happened in Israel several thousand years ago.

It is the symbolic message in this story that is important. Goliath is not just a Philistine warrior challenging the army of Israel to provide someone to take him on in single combat. He represents any threat in our lives that seems to be far beyond our ability to cope. For those of us who are growing older, this giant represents the threat of illness, loss of control and death. Brave as we may try to be in the presence of others, we know how weak and helpless we are in the privacy of our own thoughts. All this is new territory for us and we do not know how we will be able to survive in such a hostile environment.

David, a mere lad and clearly no match for the strength and experience of Goliath, represents our trust in God. Humanly speaking, it seems to be totally inadequate for the struggle that lies ahead. But we are asked to say with David, "You (the giant of fear and hopelessness) come to me with sword and spear and javelin; but I come to you in the name of the LORD of hosts, the God of the armies of Israel, whom you have defied" (1 Sam 17:45). No matter how distant God may seem to us, and no matter how little we have paid attention to him in the past, we must never doubt that God is waiting for us to call upon him in this struggle.

The whole purpose of this beautiful biblical story is to remind us that we too can stand with little David and, in the name of God, win a glorious victory over the giants that appear ahead of us. When we rely on God's help in this struggle, we will also bear witness to his goodness and power, and thus be able to join David in recognizing this fact "so that all the earth may know that there is a God in Israel" (1 Sam 17:46).

The full implications of this stunning victory of David over Goliath are not recognized until we see the connection between the victory of David and the triumph of Jesus, son of David. When David offered to fight the giant, Saul offered him armor to wear because poor Saul could think of no other way to fight than the old way—the way that would guarantee the victory of the giant. David, whose imagination was liberated by his trust in God, was able to think of the new way—the way of sling and stone—and thus to assure his victory.

In the ministry of Jesus, it appeared at first that he would be a political Messiah who would rally an army and lead Israel to victory over the hated Roman occupiers of their land. And that is surely what the people who listened to Jesus expected from him. But as Jesus pondered his mission and prayed to his Father, it became ever more clear to him that the path of violence was not the way of God. I think it was at the Transfiguration (Mark 9:2-9) that the full impact of this dawned on Jesus as he suddenly realized that God would save the world through him, not in the old, failed way of warfare but in the new, promising way of love and sacrifice and final self-offering.

Just as David had found the new way with stone and sling, so also did the Son of David find the new way of unconditional love to conquer the ultimate giant of sin and death. It certainly did not appear that this would be successful, and it still does not appear so, but the resurrection of Jesus is clear evidence that he has in fact conquered the ultimate giant. We know this through faith, and as we prepare to do battle with the giants in our future we must rely on that faith and allow it to make us courageous and confident.

We must believe that the threats that darken our future will be dispelled as surely as the giant was defeated by David and as surely as the final giant of sin and guilt and fear was defeated by Jesus. "When the Philistines saw that their champion was dead, they fled" (1 Sam 17:51). And just as surely the forces that frighten us will melt away as God's love is victorious in our lives.

20

TRUSTING GOD'S INFINITE LOVE

And just as Moses lifted up the serpent in the wilderness, so must the Son of Man be lifted up, that whoever believes in him may have eternal life. For God so loved the world that he gave his only Son, so that everyone who believes in him may not perish but may have eternal life. Indeed, God did not send the Son into the world to condemn the world, but in order that the world might be saved through him (John 3:14-17).

Everyone who watches sports programs on television will remember John 3:16. In former times especially, that reference used to appear behind home plate at the World Series and behind Arnie Palmer as he teed off at the Masters. And it is certainly a very special and very comforting text.

However, it is important to see it in its context and to probe more closely its meaning for us. According to verses fourteen and fifteen, when the Israelites were afflicted by some mysterious ailment on their desert journey, Moses was commanded to lift a bronze serpent up for all to see, and those who looked upon it with faith in the power of God would be cured (Numbers 21:6-9). John sees in this event a prefiguring of the lifting up of Jesus in crucifixion. All of us who look upon this sacrifice and understand its meaning and live that meaning will also be healed of our sinfulness.

Therefore, those who now look upon him with faith in God's power to save will not just be cured of some physical ailment but will receive liberation from the ultimate disease of sin and death. But this happens only for the person "who believes in him." The same promise is made in 3:16 where we hear of God's desire to give us life through Jesus but, once again, only on condition that we believed in him.

It should be obvious, therefore, that the whole meaning of the text is centered in the meaning of "believing" in Jesus. "Believing" can mean many things. For example, I can believe that Jesus existed, that he worked miracles in Galilee, that he died on Calvary and that he rose from the dead, but this is not the kind of believing that is meant in this text. For I can believe that all those things happened and still not change my own way of living.

When John's gospel talks about believing, it means that the one who believes not only accepts as true the fact that Jesus died for us out of love but also the conclusion that the believer also must be radically changed. We, who so often tend to be self-centered, must now realize that we should not only see and admire how unselfish Jesus was but that we should also make that ideal the first priority in our own lives. With this in mind, we can paraphrase the text of 3:16 as follows: "God so loved the world that he gave his only Son, so that all those who believe in him and make his unselfish love part of their own lives may not perish but may have eternal life."

One may memorize the Bible and attend church faithfully every Sunday and still remain an insensitive, thoughtless and domineering person. The Bible surely must be revered and going to church is a commendable thing to do, but none of this can take the place of being a loving, caring, sensitive person in the home or in the field or at the office. Reading the Bible and attending church and frequenting the sacraments will help us to be more like Jesus but none of that can replace the kind of loving that we see in Jesus and that we must express in our daily lives.

It is only too easy to imagine a situation where people are very pious on Sunday morning but then become examples of road rage the next morning on the way to work. Or teachers may be very competent but have little concern for the personal problems of their students. Or preachers may speak eloquently but are often not available in times of need. Or older persons thumb the rosary faithfully but give a hard time to all who care for them. Unfortunately, it is only too easy to add to this list.

This does not mean that we are all hypocrites or that we never practice what we preach. It simply means that we must recognize that the way to follow Jesus is to do our best to be a loving, caring presence in our world. God does not expect us to be perfect, but he would like us to try to be as much like his Son as possible. We need to take seriously what Jesus says in the verse that follows 3:16: "Indeed, God did not send his Son into the world to condemn the world, but in order that the world might be saved through him." God is more than ready to help us to be more thoughtful and sensitive and God very much wants to give us that "eternal life" which we want so much to enjoy with him and with all our friends.

21

NOURISHMENT FOR ETERNAL LIFE

Then (Jesus) was led up by the Spirit into the wilderness to be tempted by the devil. He fasted forty days and forty nights, and afterwards he was famished. The tempter came and said to him, "If you are the Son of God, command these stones to become loaves of bread." But he answered, "It is written, 'One does not live by bread alone, but by every word that comes from the mouth of God'" (Matt 4:1-4).

It is no accident that the temptation of Jesus took place immediately after his baptism. In his baptism, he was affirmed by his heavenly Father and sent on his messianic mission of salvation. Just as our own baptism commits us to make the journey traced out by Jesus, so does the baptism of Jesus commit him to his own mission. Moreover, as soon as one takes on such a commitment, doubts and hesitations will begin to arise and will provide temptations to abandon a course, which is now seen to be more difficult than expected.

It is said that Jesus was "led up by the Spirit into the wilderness" because it is the Spirit of God that accompanies both Jesus and us on our respective journeys in response to God's call. This happens "in the wilderness" because that is where Israel was tempted after their liberation from the bondage of the Pharaoh. And Jesus is said to have fasted there for "forty days" just as Israel spent forty years in the wilderness but disobeyed God and did not "fast" from sin. Jesus is, in fact, reversing the story of Israel's journey in the Sinai wilderness.

When we read this story of Jesus' temptation, we must not imagine the presence of a tempter in red long johns with horns and a tail! This tempter is the "devil" (Luke 4:3), which in Greek means a "deceiver," an understanding that is confirmed by John's gospel where we are told that the devil is "a liar and the father of lies" (8:44). The point is that Jesus is faced with deceptive suggestions which are very attractive but which will ultimately lead to disappointment and tragedy. The same is true of us.

The first of these deceptive suggestions concerns nourishment for a hungry person. Jesus is "hungry" for the fulfillment of his difficult mission and the devil suggests that he should use his miraculous powers to satisfy that hunger. But this would be simply a quick pay-off to avoid the long-term demands of his journey. In most cases, the length and the weariness of the journey are more difficult than any particular obstacle on the way.

It is not hard for us older Christians to identify with Jesus as he is tempted to cut the journey short and to settle for an immediate pay-off. Patience and perseverance are very difficult virtues and they are needed in old age perhaps more than in the busy days of our earlier years. And so we must listen carefully to the response of Jesus to this temptation: "It is written, 'One does not live by bread alone.'" Jesus is referring to the story of Israel's journey through the wilderness when they clamored for bread (see Exodus 16:3). He is reversing their impatience by rejecting this suggestion of the devil.

The text continues, "but by every word that comes from the mouth of God." This word that comes from the mouth of God is nothing less than the divine revelation about the end of the journey which for Jesus will be resurrection and glory in the kingdom of his heavenly Father. We too must be willing to stay the course and to trust the promises of God. Those who do not trust God's ways will sometimes listen to the siren song of assisted suicide. But life and death are the sacred province of God and it is a serious mistake to attempt to interfere with the plan of God who surely knows what is best for all of us.

The devil also tells Jesus that he can have all the kingdoms of the earth if he will only give up his mission and pay homage to him and to his lies. Of course, the devil is lying when he says that he can give him all earthly power. In fact, the devil can promise only the ultimate defeat that he himself experienced, as Luke makes clear when he says, "I watched Satan fall from heaven like a flash of lightning" (10:18).

Then Jesus is told to tempt God by throwing himself from the pinnacle of the temple, thus attempting to force God to intervene in favor of his Messiah. But Jesus will have none of that either, saying, "Do not put the Lord your God to the test" (Matthew 4:7). There is no doubt that some of our most ferocious temptations will occur when we are old but this is also an opportunity to show our trust in God's goodness—a trust that will be rewarded beyond our wildest dreams.

22

YEARNING FOR GOD'S PRESENCE

How lovely is your dwelling place, O LORD of hosts! My soul longs, indeed it faints for the courts of the LORD; my heart and my flesh sing for joy to the living God... For a day in your courts is better than a thousand elsewhere (Ps 84:1-2,10).

We modern human beings are incredibly footloose and fancy free when it comes to a domicile. In this respect, we stand in sharp contrast to our ancestors, most of whom never ventured out of the valley or plain of their birth to seek adventure in a larger world. But we do have a quality in common with them. No matter how much we roam, we have a special place where we feel completely at home.

This precious place of refuge may be our physical home, although in a world of so much domestic strife and dissention, that may unfortunately be a place that we would rather avoid. The place of peace and security is so cherished that we dream about it when we are far away and we relax and rejoice whenever we come to it again. It may be a rustic cabin in the mountains or a place by the seashore or just a spot that has been hallowed by memories of childhood freedom and joy.

The psalmist celebrates such a place in his own life. He has found this place, not by wandering far and wide, but by gazing ever more deeply into the center of his being where he finds the hidden presence of God. This is a familiar God whom he has visited many times before and in whom he finds the object of his greatest desires. Of course, in the psalm he recognizes this special place of meeting with God in the Jerusalem temple. But he has learned that if God is not found deep inside his heart, he will not be found anywhere else—not even in the most beautiful and elaborate shrine.

Nonetheless, there is such a resonance between the God of his heart and the God of the temple that it is a special joy to bring the two forms of presence together and to celebrate them in the sacred songs and joyful festive liturgy of God's house. We are all creatures made up of body and spirit and we need the support of visual and audible expressions of our joy in God's presence. We also need the support of those who gather with us on such occasions.

The psalmist tells us that his "soul longs, indeed it faints for the courts of the Lord." To be in love always means to live with an aching heart for we never achieve the perfect union that love seeks. If this is true of human relationships, it is much truer of our relationship of love with God. All the mystics complain about what seems to be the will-o'-the wisp nature of God as he relates to us human beings. This is also a constant theme of that great biblical love story, the Song of Songs.

As we grow older, and perhaps a little wiser, we become painfully aware of the experience in our lives of a radical sense of incompleteness. We learn what St. Augustine meant when he wrote that the human heart remains forever restless until it finally rests in God. Like the salmon, we are programmed to return to the source of our being and we can never find real peace until that is achieved. This is a very healthy situation in the realm of the spirit and one of the best prayers we can ever say is to tell God that we yearn and pine for the wonderful homecoming that he has prepared for us.

When children away at school return home for vacation, a loving mother prepares their favorite meal. God wants to do the same for us. Then we will be able to say with the psalmist, "a day in your courts is better than a thousand elsewhere." Our own relationship with God may not be nearly as personal as that of the psalmist. But we must not be discouraged. We can be sure that the psalmist did not arrive at this happy condition without much prayer and yearning. The important thing for us to remember is that God wants this kind of relationship with us even more than we do. We must simply be patient and wish for it with all our heart.

In fact, Jesus himself tells us this when he tells the story of the poor widow and the unjust judge (Luke 18:3-8). At first the judge is not interested but the woman persists and he finally relents. Jesus comments: "Listen to what the unjust judge says. And will not God grant justice to his chosen ones who cry to him day and night" (Luke 18:6-7)? The wonderful experience of God's presence in our hearts is indeed something to be prayed for day and night.

as loving parent and to yearn to be taken into his strong arms. If one's face is "ashamed" because of the awareness of past sins and shortcomings, this will all be changed at the sight of God smiling on us with forgiveness. The sun of God's face will easily conquer the sadness and hesitation in our own faces.

A few verses later, the psalmist invites us to "taste and see that the Lord is good." The sense of taste helps us to determine whether something we eat is really good for us. It savors and evaluates the food we put into our mouths. As such, it expresses to a high degree what is usually meant by experience. Its judgment is based, not on hearsay nor the label on the package, but on the actual response of our taste buds. We are accustomed to saying that "the proof of the pudding is in the eating," but that surely means that the test is especially in the tasting.

We are invited, therefore, to move beyond hearsay and titles and labels to an immediate and personal experience of the goodness and mercy of that dear Lord who has not hesitated to give his life for us. God wants us to know Jesus in this experiential way and is ready, therefore, to embrace us if we only decide to reach out to him.

All of this is especially true when we grow older and realize that we cannot and need not try to manage everything by ourselves. After inviting us to taste the goodness of the Lord, the psalmist declares that those are "happy who take refuge in him." In other words, we are told that seeking the arms of the Lord is not an admission of defeat; rather, it is finding a safe harbor at the end of a long journey.

God's arms are truly extended toward us and we are urged to find refuge and peace and joy in the embrace of our loving creator. "Taste and see that the LORD is good." Do not rely on what others may say. For each one of us, "tasting" the Lord is a very personal and unique experience. We do this most effectively when we engage in quiet prayer. The Lord wants to be savored by us and there is no danger that this will ever become a routine experience. Savoring the Lord by keeping him always in our thoughts will become more enjoyable and more fruitful the longer we do it.

The best way to pray in this manner is to sit quietly and to ask God quite simply, "Lord, tell me what I need to know." And as we listen intently, God will tell us in a thousand wordless ways what he told his beloved Son at his baptism, "You are my beloved Son, in whom I am well pleased." When addressed to us, the words will be, "You are my beloved child; I love you more than you will ever know." When we hear these words, spoken to our hearts, we will know what tasting and savoring the Lord really means. And when that happens, all fear and anxiety will be driven from our hearts.

We live in a world where we are bombarded by words and sometimes we can be very confused about what we really need to hear. At such times, we need to remember that the only words that we absolutely, positively must hear are those affirming, loving words of our heavenly Father calling us his beloved children. We won't be able to make it through life successfully if we fail to hear that message; we will make it easily if we do hear those words and take them to heart.

29

CALMING THE STORMS IN OUR HEARTS

A wind storm arose on the sea, so great that the boat was being swamped by the waves; but (Jesus) was asleep. And they went and woke him up, saying, "Lord, save us! We are perishing!" And he said to them, "Why are you afraid, you of little faith?" Then he got up and rebuked the winds and the sea; and there was a dead calm. They were amazed, saying, "What sort of man is this, that even the winds and the sea obey him?" (Matt 8:24-27).

There are few experiences more frightening than to be in a small boat on a lake during a thunderstorm or a sudden squall. And there is good reason for fear because one is in imminent danger of drowning. Even though the disciples of Jesus were accustomed to working on the Sea of Galilee, or perhaps because they were so accustomed, they knew the grave danger they were in and had every reason to cry out, "Lord, save us! We are perishing!"

When the evangelist tells us that Jesus was asleep during all this, it does not imply that he had some supernatural knowledge that made him aware that everything would be alright. The fact is that Jesus was not himself a fisherman and may not have fully realized the plight they were in. But we must also realize that this story was written long after the event and the author wants us, who are like the disciples, to understand that Jesus is a source of calm and serenity in all the chaotic situations of human life.

Jesus is speaking to all of us, therefore, when he says to the frightened disciples, "Why are you afraid, you of little faith?" I don't think Jesus is suggesting that we should never be afraid of anything. That would be almost impossible for fragile human beings. But he does want us to understand that we should not feel so helpless that we are paralyzed by fear. And the reason is that we have someone to whom we can turn—someone who loves us and is very powerful.

Our secular culture bombards us incessantly with advice about how to become self-sufficient. But that is a foolish illusion. It is true that we should try to stand on our own two feet and manage our own affairs, but total self-sufficiency is far beyond our abilities. We need other people, and they need us, and all of us together need God. There is nothing unworthy or demeaning about this. In fact, it makes a loving community possible and thus makes life a wonderful experience of mutual love and support.

When we are young and strong and self-confident, it may seem to us that self-sufficiency is a possibility for human beings. But as we grow older and accumulate some experience of life, it becomes ever more obvious that we cannot cope with all the trials of life by ourselves. There are so many areas of our lives where we have no real control over what happens. And yet our happiness and peace depend to a large extent on what is happening in those areas. Our loved ones are often in danger, our own health is often uncertain, our nation is sometimes in turmoil. We can indeed feel like those disciples in their small fishing boat being tossed about by a violent and uncontrollable storm.

And that is why the gospel story is focused on Jesus and on what he is willing and able to do for his disciples, and for us. "Then he got up and rebuked the winds and the sea; and there was a dead calm" (Matt 8:26). We can almost feel the sudden change from terrible fear and anxiety to wonderful peace and serenity. I'm sure that we have all had this experience of incredible relief and relaxation after an especially worrisome and frightening experience. The sigh that comes from deep inside us is so real and so personal that we want to sit very still and savor the peace and security that it implies.

But what about the times when the winds do not die down and the storm continues to rage? The medical news we awaited may not be good and our fear and anxiety may not be eased. In some mysterious way, this is precisely when the miraculous calming of the storm can really happen. For the storm in our hearts can also be calmed by a loving God who gives us the ability to accept whatever happens with trust and confidence.

We see how this happened in the case of Jesus himself. He had survived many trials and threats but in the garden of Gethsemane his heavenly Father told him that the final trial could not be postponed. The reaction of Jesus was to accept this decision in total trust: "Abba, Father, for you all things are possible; remove this cup from me; yet, not what I want, but what you want" (Mark 14:36). Jesus then moved quickly to the climax of his life and the storm blew away and the sun came out on that glorious Easter morning.

Jesus asks us to trust him so much that we can join the disciples in exclaiming, "What sort of man is this, that even the winds and the sea obey him." But it will mean so much more when we join Jesus in final glory.

30

GOD ALWAYS HEARS OUR PRAYERS

*So I say to you, Ask, and it will be given you; search, and
you will find; knock, and the door will be opened for you. For
everyone who asks receives, and everyone who searches finds,
and for everyone who knocks, the door will be opened. Is there
anyone among you who, if your child asks for a fish, will give a
snake instead of a fish? Or if the child asks for an egg, will give
a scorpion? If you then, who are evil, know how to give good
gifts to your children, how much more will the heavenly Father
give the Holy Spirit to those who ask him* (Luke 11:9-13)!

The most distinctive feature of Luke's gospel is the great
journey that Jesus makes from Galilee to Jerusalem, beginning
in 9:51 and not ending until 19:40. This is a spiritual journey
and is intended to be a model for our own journey through life.
In the course of this journey, Jesus tells us what our priorities
should be if we hope to be ready for the final sacrifice in our
own Jerusalem and for the victory that follows if we have been
faithful to the wisdom taught by Jesus.

It is not surprising, therefore, to learn that an essential element in this journey is prayer. For praying is like breathing, and

we cannot possibly make this journey, through dark valleys and over high mountains, without drawing in that life sustaining air. And as we grow older this becomes even more important, for the highest mountains will usually be found at the end of the journey.

In the passage quoted, Luke seems to be saying something that is not at all in accord with our own experience. For we can remember many occasions when we asked and did not receive, or searched and did not find, or discovered that the doors did not open to us. Nonetheless, our prayers are never unnoticed or unanswered, even if God bides his time or responds in ways we do not recognize. Those who have been parents will recall how often their children asked for things that were not good for them, or for which they were not yet ready.

And it is precisely from the perspective of a parent that Jesus goes on to point out how we would never give a child a snake for a fish or a scorpion for an egg. (Scorpions in Israel are white and just about the size of an egg). In fact, we are almost offended just to hear such a suggestion. But the conclusion drawn by Jesus is immensely comforting.

"If you then, who are evil, know how to give good gifts to your children, how much more will the heavenly Father give the Holy Spirit to those who ask him!" Jesus is not really accusing us of being evil; the point is that, by comparison with God, we are far less holy, even aside from sinfulness. But if we know how to respond to difficulties in a positive way, how much more will God do the same.

We should pay special attention to how it is that God will respond to our prayers. Jesus does not say that God will give us everything we ask for, even when it is an obviously good thing. Rather, he will give us "the Holy Spirit." In other words, God will give us his own Spirit to guide us on this journey of life. The Spirit will help us to make wise decisions in troubling situations. But, most of all, the Holy Spirit will turn our attention away from earthly and passing things to the heavenly Father, who awaits us with open arms.

I have often thought that one of the most important things that the Holy Spirit can do for us is to make us homesick for God. Homesickness can be a very painful experience. I recall vividly my first year away from home. I was just going on thirteen when I went away to a boarding high school. After Christmas vacation I was so homesick that I could hardly keep the tears from showing. I told my classmates that I had a terrible cold! Later on, I realized that I was very fortunate to have the kind of home for which I could yearn so desperately.

In the journey of life, it is very easy to become so engrossed in our own affairs that we almost forget God entirely. But the fact is that he made us and loves us and really wants us to come to him as often as possible with all our concerns and requests. God's love for us is like a powerful magnet that draws us toward the future and toward our true homeland. As we grow older, we need to remember this and to allow ourselves to feel the pull of that magnet. As we do this, we will begin to understand that "the best is still to come," and that there is "no place like home," especially when it is our heavenly home.

31

WITH GOD WE CAN
CONQUER GIANTS

Moses sent them to spy out the land of Canaan…. And they told him, "We came to the land to which you sent us; it flows with milk and honey…. Yet the people who live in the land are strong, and the towns are fortified and very large… and all the people that we saw in it are of great size…. Then all the congregation raised a loud cry, and the people wept that night. And all the Israelites complained against Moses and Aaron; the whole congregation said to them, "Would that we had died in the land of Egypt" (Num 13:17, 27-28, 32; 14:1-2).

We recall that Moses led the Hebrew slaves out of Egypt with such power and might that their euphoria knew no bounds. All this is captured in Psalm 114: "When Israel went out from Egypt…the sea looked and fled;… the mountains skipped like rams, the hills like lambs" (1, 3-4). Even the ponderous mountains had to join in the celebration. But that was then!

Just a few years later, we find the Israelites frightened, discouraged and rebellious. They have been plodding through the desert under the leadership of Moses and Aaron. Their hopes of entering the Promised Land of Canaan directly from the south have been dashed by the report of scouts sent to spy out the land.

These scouts return with glowing reports about the beauty and fertility of the land. It is a veritable paradise of "milk and honey," i.e. everything that hungry desert dwellers could ever hope for. That was the good news. But the bad news cancelled all their joyful observations. For the land was protected by fortified cities whose inhabitants were "of great size;" they seemed like giants. In fact, the scouts embellished their account by noting that they themselves by comparison "seemed like grasshoppers" (13:33). And so, with hopes dashed, the people complained bitterly to Moses and Aaron, and even asked to return to Egyptian bondage.

As we grow older, it is only too easy for us to identify with these discouraged Israelites. This is especially true on our "bad days" when our bodies are hurting and our hearts are heavy. We too have heard from the biblical "scouts" who have gone before us that heaven is a wonderful place, where we will find all that our hearts could desire after the long and difficult journey of this life.

But there are other voices too. And they warn us about the terrible problems that lie ahead of us. These are "of great size, veritable giants," and we cannot hope to deal with them. Who are these giants? They are all the possible forms of illness and disability and dependence on others...and then the frightening prospect of total helplessness and death. Indeed, there are problems of gigantic proportion looming in our future, as some would have us imagine it. But that is only what the prophets of doom and gloom have to say.

We must attune our ears to other voices. They tell us that most of the dire predictions that we hear will never come to pass and so it is wasted time to worry about them. They also tell us, as Josue and Caleb told the Israelites: "If the Lord is pleased with us, he will bring us into this land and give it to us, a land that flows with milk and honey" (Num 14:8). Then these trusting scouts tell us the secret of their optimism: "the lord is with us; do not fear them" (Num 14:9).

When we are assailed with doubts and fears, we must counter the poison of doom and gloom by repeating over and over again, "The lord is with us; do not fear them." This is the best medicine that we could ever take and it has the power to overcome even the most fearsome spiritual ailments that we might experience.

Those among the Israelites who took this kind of medicine, as prescribed by their divine physician, did in fact enter the Promised Land and thus learned to praise and thank the Lord: "(God) sustained (Israel) in a desert land, in a howling wilderness waste; he shielded him, cared for him, guarded him as the apple of his eye" (Deut 32:10). If the Lord is with us, we have nothing to fear. "So Israel lives in safety, untroubled is Jacob's abode in a land of grain and wine, where the heavens drop down dew" (Deut 33:28).

As we grow older, it is not difficult for us to look ahead and to see there "a howling wilderness waste." This pessimism is captured in the words, "Well, he or she isn't really going to get better." From the worldly perspective of physical wellbeing and comfort, this is a statement of reality. But there is so much more to life than simply feeling well or being productive. Now is the time for witnessing to God's love and goodness, in spite of everything.

32

FAITH CONQUERS ALL

And these signs will accompany those who believe: by using my name they will cast out demons; they will speak in new tongues; they will pick up snakes in their hands, and if they drink any deadly thing, it will not hurt them; they will lay their hands on the sick, and they will recover (Mark 16:17-18).

It is very likely that most of us who read the gospel of Mark are puzzled by this passage which occurs near the end of that gospel. There are some who take these words literally and actually handle poisonous snakes in religious services. I think that most reasonable people would consider that practice to be out of harmony with what Mark really wants to convey with these words. And yet, if they should not be taken literally, what are we to make of them?

I am convinced that Mark is here using metaphorical language to warn us about the dangers that exist on the journey of faith that will hopefully bring us to the heavenly kingdom. Thus, "casting out demons" would not be the use of exorcisms, but rather the exposure and rejection of those false promises that claim to provide health and happiness but which really bring demonic chaos into our lives. After all, when Jesus drove out demons, he was challenging those forces from the original chaos, which God conquered in order to bring order and harmony into the universe. Though conquered by the Creator, these forces still try to destroy order in the world. They do so through false promises which include all the nostrums that promise salvation without true conversion to unselfish behavior.

Authentic believers will also "speak in new tongues." Since they use the name of Jesus, their old, negative language of fear and anxiety will be replaced by the language of hope and optimism. This phenomenon could include the speaking in tongues that we hear about in Paul's First Letter to the Corinthians (e.g. 12:10), because that gift of the Spirit is also about bearing witness to the hope that Christ has given us. To dare to speak in new tongues about the hope and promise that God has offered us is surely one of the most obvious characteristics of real Christians. Young people seem to be hopeful because their lives lie before them; as we grow older we have little reason to speak so hopefully except that we firmly believe in the promise that Jesus has offered us. When we bear such witness, we become beacons of light for the whole community.

I believe that the handling of snakes and the drinking of something poisonous are to be understood metaphorically also. They represent examples of the dangers that in the ancient world threatened those on a journey. Travelers needed to be alert for snakes that might strike from the side of an unfamiliar path and they learned early in life that death could easily follow after drinking from an unknown well. Typhoid is usually spread by water and those who drank from wells in their own villages had become immune (or had already died) from that domestic strain of typhoid. But they were not protected from the poisonous germs in other wells. Of course, Mark is not giving a lesson in how to avoid typhoid. Rather, snakes and disease symbolize the dangers that threaten those who make the journey of faith, notably, cynicism and despair.

Surely there are no dangers in life that are so destructive as are negative and bitter attitudes about life and about the future. Such a spiritual virus is infectious and threatens the hope of many other people also. I think that older persons especially are tempted to turn negative and to look for danger everywhere rather than to trust in God and to speak positively about the future. There are few sights that are sadder than the example of an old person who has become bitter about life, just as older people with vibrant hope are a wonderful witness to the promises of God.

Finally, the true believers will lay hands upon the sick and make them well. I do not think that Mark is referring here to what we call faith healing. That is something that may be present in a Christian community, but I believe that the reference here is to something more common. If we have ever been in a hospital, we will remember how helpful it was when visitors spoke to us in hopeful terms.

Those who use a hospital visit to tell us about their own medical problems or to remind us that someone else has died from our malady are not "laying on hands" and encouraging recovery. A positive and spiritually healthy doctor, nurse or visitor can work wonders for those who are ill and perhaps frightened in the strange environment of the hospital.

Mark thus offers us a golden text that illuminates our journey of faith, and never more so than when we have already walked a long way on the journey from birth to final victory in Jesus. It is the poisonous snake of cynicism and the poisonous drink of despair that we must avoid at all cost. We must strive instead to live in the light and joy of God's promises.

33

THE SPIRIT IS OUR BEST TEACHER

If you love me, you will keep my commandments. And I will ask the Father, and he will give you another Advocate, to be with you forever. This is the Spirit of truth, whom the world cannot receive, because it neither sees him nor knows him. You know him, because he abides with you, and he will be in you…. But the Advocate, the Holy Spirit, whom the Father will send in my name, will teach you everything, and remind you of all that I have said to you (John 14:15-17, 26).

Jesus tells us that we will be able to keep his "commandments" to love God and to love one another only on condition that we have come to know him in such a deeply personal and intuitive way that he becomes the very center of our lives. In this case, we will make no significant decisions without thinking also of his wishes and of the ideal of unselfish love that he has taught us. It is as if there is a seat reserved for God in every discussion about the way in which we should lead our lives.

However, we may still feel weak and unable to live fully the ideal of unselfishness. That is why Jesus promises to ask the Father to send "another Advocate" who will live with us and give us the power to do what we could never do by our own efforts. The first Advocate is Jesus himself, as we learn from 1 John 2:1: "But if anyone does sin, we have an advocate with the Father, Jesus Christ the righteous." Thus we have two powerful allies who will plead our case before the heavenly Father.

Jesus then tells us that this Advocate is the "Spirit of truth." In John's gospel, this means that the Spirit has a perfect understanding of the revelation that Jesus has brought to us from his Father. This sublime revelation is that the Father loves us more than we can ever understand and that we are asked to make that love present in our world by trying to love others in the same unselfish way. Paul understands the role of the Spirit in much the same way when he writes: "These things God has revealed to us through the Spirit; for the Spirit searches everything, even the depth of God" (1 Cor 2:10).

Those who belong to the secular and unbelieving world cannot receive this Spirit because they are unwilling to give up their quest for selfish interests. They have fallen under the spell of the devil, the great Deceiver, who suggests to them that power and control are all that matter in life. Their fixation on their own interests blinds them to the possibility of another and better way to live. That is why Jesus calls the devil "a liar and the father of lies" (John 8:44). In the end, it is only the apparent foolishness of love and concern for others that will matter.

By contrast, those who believe in Jesus' message of love and service will welcome the Advocate/Spirit. They will have an instinctive recognition of the presence of the Spirit in their lives and will know intuitively what they should do in order to make the love of Jesus a reality in their lives. As we say sometimes, they will not have to think twice about what the love of Jesus in their lives will mean in even the most difficult situations.

Jesus goes on to say that this Holy Spirit will teach us everything and will explain for us the meaning of what he has said and done during his life among us. This not only means that the Spirit will be with the Church as her teachers explain the Scriptures; it also assures us that we can all rely on the Spirit to tell us how to be like Jesus in all the circumstances of our lives. This is especially important for us older folks who cannot see how Jesus might have dealt with the problems of old age since he died so young.

The Spirit will be present at the innermost center of our being to help us trust the ways of God just as Jesus trusted his heavenly Father in the garden of Gethsemane and accepted his dying as the only way to save the world. Given half a chance, this same Spirit will make clear to us the value of our resolute trust in God even as we grow weaker and must deal with much suffering. This is not something that we can reason out on our own. It will be a conviction that goes far beyond human reason and is the voice of the Spirit telling us the truth about what really counts in human life.

This is surely what Jesus means when he continues and says: "Peace I leave with you; my peace I give to you" (John 14:27). Peace, or "shalom," in the Bible does not mean simply the cessation of hostilities. It is a deep, inner conviction that God is in his heaven and all is right with the world. All is right because the Spirit is with us, come what may, and reminds us over and over again that, if we do our best to be a loving presence to others, nothing else really matters. This alone brings peace—a peace that can exist and thrive in the midst of warfare and in the midst of our own weakness and pain.

34

GOD HAS A SPECIAL LOVE
FOR THE AGED

Do not cast me off in the time of old age; do not forsake me when my strength is spent…. O God, from my youth you have taught me, and I still proclaim your wondrous deeds. So even to old age and gray hairs, O God, do not forsake me (Psalm 71:9, 17-18).

The Psalms are full of references to the adversities of our human existence but there are relatively few explicit examples of concern for the problems of old age. This is probably due to the fact that very few people in the ancient world ever came even close to what we now call old age. It is estimated that half of all infants in those days did not live to see their first birthday. And those who did survive infancy could hardly expect to live beyond middle age.

It is all the more welcome, therefore, to have a few precious Psalms that speak expressly and poignantly of the plight of the aged. Old persons know that they have outlived most of their contemporaries. They are like that proverbial "last leaf upon the tree in the spring" that Oliver Wendell Holmes wrote about. They feel that they are strangers among all these young adults and children.

Nor is the future all that promising. They have only the promises of God to console them. They hope that God will remember them: "Do not forsake me when my strength is spent." God must be very busy, and they fear that he will perhaps forget them as they come to the end of the road. We are tempted to think this way especially when our prayers seem not to be heard.

In this frame of mind, we speak to God about our past, about our histories. We have been able to live meaningful lives only because the Lord has shared his wisdom with us. One of the greatest blessings in life is to have had a good teacher—a mentor—to guide and encourage us when the world is both wonderful and dangerous. Looking back over our long lives, we can appreciate the blessing of God's instruction, especially in the revelation of the Torah, the divine law.

We all know how true it is that it is only in later years that we begin to appreciate what we owe to good teachers and wise parents. Then we can see how close we may have come to ruining our lives because of some foolish and impulsive act. Only our trust in the wisdom of older and wiser persons has kept us from folly and disappointment. Even with that help, we have made our share of mistakes! We can be happy now that we have continued to celebrate God's "wondrous deeds," in spite of God's apparent absence at times in the past.

These "wondrous deeds" of God include above all the liberation of the Hebrew slaves from the bondage of the Pharaoh, which is the source of all Old Testament revelation. But it also includes the liberation of all of us from the bondage of sin and death through the death and resurrection of Jesus, which occurred on the anniversary of the Exodus and which is the source of all New Testament revelation. We can never finish marveling at the love of God for us and at our great good fortune because that love has come into our world and is available to us every minute of every day.

The presence of God's "wondrous deeds" is guaranteed by the sacrament of the Eucharist. Every time we enter into the mystery of that sacrament, we touch again the power and love of God that brought about the miracle of the Exodus and the Resurrection. In a sense, we come right up to the edge of eternity and allow the power of God to transform a little bit of our earthly lives. When that happens, we can truly say with the psalmist, "I still proclaim your wondrous deeds."

I now recall, more vividly than ever, the "wondrous deeds" which were the unselfish love and care of my mother and father. And I recall too how my father, as he approached eighty, used to check out the obituaries and declare occasionally, "There goes another of my old buddies!" The intriguing factor in all this is the fact that he was not particularly close to some of these "old buddies." That puzzled me until I realized that he felt such a bond with them because they were his generation and, as their numbers dwindled, they became ever more precious in his eyes. In a sense, he felt that he was being isolated and forgotten.

It is for this reason that we should say often, with the psalmist, "Even to old age and gray hairs, O God, do not forsake me." We hope that God will help us to begin to think more and more about that wondrous place beyond all this where we expect to meet again our parents and grandparents…and all our "old buddies," even if we weren't too close to them.

35

THE FREELY CHOSEN VULNERABILITY OF JESUS

For I received from the Lord what I also handed on to you, that the Lord Jesus on the night when he was betrayed took a loaf of bread, and when he had given thanks, he broke it and said, "This is my body that is for you. Do this in remembrance of me." In the same way he took the cup also, after supper, saying, "This cup is the new covenant in my blood. Do this, as often as you drink it, in remembrance of me. For as often as you eat this bread and drink the cup, you proclaim the Lord's death until he comes" (1 Cor 11:23-26).

It is important that we recall the context of Paul's account of the institution of the Eucharist. At that time, the Eucharist was accompanied by a kind of covered dish supper as a sign of mutual love and support in the community. Paul is very disturbed to learn that some of the wealthier members of the community are bringing food of better quality and are not putting it on the common table but are eating it by themselves. Such behavior is completely contrary to the meaning of the Eucharist, which is the central Christian expression of mutual love and support.

In such a pastoral context, Paul reminds his readers of the spirit in which Jesus instituted this sacrament at the Last Supper. For this spirit was the antithesis of the natural human tendency to hoard and compete in all aspects of life. Jesus made himself totally vulnerable when he offered his body and blood for the nourishment of us very needy human beings. He said, "This is my body that is for you." He thus declared that his body and his very being are not objects to be protected at all cost but that they are freely given so that others may have life.

It was Jesus' experience of his heavenly Father's love that gave him the freedom to make such a generous sacrifice. He wants us also to reject our tendency to "collect and protect" as we become ever more vulnerable to the needs of others. Our participation in the Eucharist becomes a powerful reminder of this ideal. But it also reminds us of the love of the Father for us—a love that can liberate us and enable us to reproduce the love of Jesus in our own circumstances.

In the gospel story of the Last Supper, there is always a reference to the betrayal of Jesus by Judas, one of that intimate group that followed Jesus in his ministry. This recalls no doubt an historical and tragic fact, but it seems to have a deeper purpose than that. I am personally convinced that the emphasis placed on the betrayal of Jesus is meant to remind us that the experience of betrayal is almost inseparable from the willingness to love to the point of vulnerability.

In other words, if we are so cautious in loving that we cannot be hurt, it may very well be a sign that our loving is not as generous as it should be. We may think it is an ideal to be able to say that we have never allowed anyone to break through our armor to the point of being really hurt. While we must not be so unguarded that we can be hurt by anyone, it is surely even more tragic to be so protective of our hearts that we can never experience real hurt. The love of Jesus was so generous that it almost invited betrayal.

We will never know just how guilty the historical Judas may have been, but Judas as a symbolic figure is a powerful reminder of our need to be such loving persons that an occasional feeling of being betrayed is not unexpected. The reaction of Jesus to his own betrayal reminds us that forgiveness is the only proper answer to the terrible experience of betrayal. There is profound sadness, but no anger, in the response of Jesus to the kiss of Judas: "Judas, is it with a kiss that you are betraying the Son of Man" (Luke 22:48)? We older folks need to be particularly aware of this because we can easily hang on to old hurts for no good purpose.

We must pay attention also to the final words of Jesus in this passage: "For as often as you eat this bread and drink the cup, you proclaim the Lord's death until he comes." Through these words, Paul makes it very clear that we should continue to celebrate the Lord's supper as a sacramental way of participating in this central event in the life of Jesus. But he also tells us that we must do much more than merely recall this event. Whenever we participate in the celebration of the Eucharist, we are "proclaiming," i.e. making a strong statement, about the meaning of "the Lord's death." For it is the death of Jesus, much more than his resurrection, that expresses the unconditional love that brought our salvation. The resurrection is merely the glorious celebration of that victory of love over every kind of evil. And as we proclaim this fact, we also are made conscious that the same kind of unselfish love must characterize our own daily lives.

36

TRUSTING GOD IS A WONDERFUL INVESTMENT

Hoping against hope, (Abraham) believed that he would become "the father of many nations"...He did not weaken in faith when he considered his own body, which was already as good as dead (for he was about a hundred years old), or when he considered the barrenness of Sarah's womb. No distrust made him waver concerning the promise of God, but he grew strong in his faith as he gave glory to God, being fully convinced that God was able to do what he had promised (Rom 4:18-21).

In the first chapters of his letter to the Romans, Paul writes about the terrible burden of sin that prevents us from achieving the promise of life and joy that God holds for us. His conclusion is that it is only faith that can lift that weight from our shoulders and allow us to run unhindered on the path of life. This faith is a gift of God but we must be willing to embrace it and to allow it to free us for loving service as we trust firmly in the promise it offers.

Like a good teacher, Paul looks for an example to illustrate the power of faith in our fragile human lives. Not surprisingly, he remembers Abraham, the great patriarch of Israel, whose life was one long and continuous roller-coaster ride as he tried to deal with the terrible contrast between God's glorious promise of innumerable posterity and the reality of a childless marriage. In those days, before there was any concept of meaningful life after death, one's posterity was the only kind of immortality available. Thus, to die childless was apparently to die forever.

Nonetheless, Abraham and Sarah clung to the hope that somehow God would fulfill his promise of a numberless posterity and thus give joy to their old age and allow them to die in the midst of loving children and grandchildren. At the same time, the reality of death was all around them. When Abraham dared to look at his ninety-nine year old body, he saw nothing there that gave him any hope or consolation. And when he thought about Sarah, who was a relatively youthful ninety (!), he could hardly have imagined any possibility of childbirth. So there they were, hoping for new life and surrounded on every side by the signs of death.

However, St. Paul declares with obvious admiration: "No distrust made him waver concerning the promise of God, being fully convinced that God was able to do what he had promised." Under the circumstances, such a conviction is nothing less than a miracle. And the danger is that we too will simply call it a miracle and dismiss it as irrelevant to our own lives. If such were the case, the biblical author would never have bothered to record it. For the fact is that the victory of the faith of Abraham and Sarah is presented to us as a model for us. There may be some exaggeration about the age of these biblical figures in order to make the point more dramatically. But the real lesson is that God has promised unending life to every one of us, and we can be robbed of this blessed gift only if we fail to trust God's goodness and faithfulness, no matter how desperate our situation may seem to be.

When we are young and strong, this divine promise of eternal life doesn't seem to matter all that much. We are so full of energy and there are so many challenges that we have little time to think about such matters. But when our energy begins to leave us, and even trifocals and cataract surgery don't help too much with the fine print, then we need to examine the quality of our faith and the depth of our trust in God's promises. Can we say then, as Paul said about Abraham, that no distrust makes us waver concerning the promise of God, being fully convinced that God is able to do what he has promised?

I think that we should look upon this challenge as the ultimate and most perfect opportunity to praise God. For surely, if we really think about this, we will discover that trust is the most beautiful gift that we can give to another person. And I'm sure that God must feel the same way about that.

When Paul said that Abraham grew strong in his faith, he also said that, by doing so "he gave glory to God." In our later years, therefore, we have this blessed opportunity to praise God by trusting his goodness. This will enable us to be more hopeful and more patient…and perhaps even to smile a little in expectation of the fulfillment of that promise.

We don't have to live long to discover that without trust in God's goodness and mercy we will not be able to survive. Abraham and Sarah trusted God and this tells us that we can do the same. This can make all the difference in our lives…and there is nothing more beautiful than old persons who are peaceful and confident because they trust the goodness of the Lord.

37

DYING IN CHRIST MAKES NEW LIFE POSSIBLE

Jesus answered them "The hour has come for the Son of Man to be glorified. Very truly, I tell you, unless a grain of wheat falls into the earth and dies, it remains just a single grain; but if it dies, it bears much fruit…. Whoever serves me must follow me, and where I am, there will my servant be also" (John 12:23-24, 26).

In the gospel of John, Jesus speaks frequently about a mysterious "hour" that will be the climax of his career as messianic Savior. He tells his mother at Cana that his hour has not yet come (2:4). Now, however, he tells us, for the first time in the gospel, that his hour has indeed arrived. Moreover, he tells us that this hour will be the time of his glorification.

We may be inclined to think that by glorification he means his resurrection and ascension. In John's gospel, however, the glorification of Jesus occurs at his crucifixion, for it is then that his love for us is most perfectly revealed. After all, in the Bible, glorification always refers to the manifestation of something that has been hidden. In most cases, this is an external manifestation of God's presence, as for example the luminous cloud that accompanied the Israelites when they left Egypt. In the case of Jesus' crucifixion, it is called his glorification because he is lifted up for all to see that the whole purpose of his life was to die for the love of us.

Jesus reinforces this understanding when he proceeds immediately to offer an analogy that describes perfectly what happens when he gives his life for us. Jesus' audience was made up in large part of farmers who would be able to understand what he meant when he compared himself to a grain of wheat, which gives its life so that more grains can be produced.

As a former farm boy myself, I can recall how we would sometimes pull up a stalk of wheat and see, among the roots of the plant, a dry empty husk, which was all that was left of a once solid and vital grain. But on the top of the stalk there were as many as forty or more new grains, which had come into being because the original grain had given its life for them. That original grain had no choice in the matter but, if we were to endow it with free will, we might well imagine that it would resist the moisture that made it swell and then produce a sprout and eventually more grains.

Jesus sees himself as that grain of wheat that freely offers its life for the sake of a multitude of people who would have no lasting life without him. And he challenges us to do the same. In fact, one can say without hesitation that this is the primary challenge that Jesus presents to us. It is so difficult to give one's life—one's most precious possession—so that others may live and flourish. Some do this literally as when soldiers die for their country's freedom or when firemen enter a building filled with fire. Good parents also give much of their lives for the sake of their children.

This kind of heroic behavior would be impossible if it were

not for the power of love. I have a friend who is a fairly typical American man and, when I saw him once changing his child's diaper, I looked at him with a certain amount of amazement. He saw my reaction and then said to me, "It makes a big difference when it's your own." His parental love gave him the ability to do something that he would never have imagined in the carefree days of his bachelorhood. This is true of many who have learned to love and have found that this gives them a power to sacrifice that they never realized they possessed.

But the unselfishness of so many good people in so many ordinary ways does not yet exhaust all the power of love. Jesus did many good and loving things when he cured the sick in Galilee. But that was nothing compared to the self-sacrifice that brought him to Jerusalem and to death on a cross. We too must go to Jerusalem to meet our own Calvary. This is especially true for those of us who have reached the "golden years." It takes a lot of loving and trusting to accept the weakness and loss of control that are an inevitable part of our final years.

This is our own special "hour" when we too can manifest in our lives some of that "glory of God" which Jesus prayed for and which he displayed so dramatically on the cross. In these challenging years, we will begin to understand what Jesus meant when he said, "Whoever serves me must follow me, and where I am, there my servant will be also." As we try to be positive and hopeful, in spite of everything, and as we try not to be a burden to others, we will truly be followers of Jesus, who was happy to imitate that empty hull of wheat so that we all might live forever.

38

GOD'S SPECIAL CONCERN FOR THE ELDERLY

Listen to me, O house of Jacob, all the remnant of the house of Israel, who have been borne by me from your birth, carried from the womb; even to your old age I am he, even when you turn gray I will carry you. I have made, and I will bear; I will carry and will save…. I have spoken, and I will bring it to pass; I have planned, and I will do it (Isa 46:3-4, 11).

After the death of Solomon, Israel entered a period of political division between the northern ten tribes and the two southern tribes. The northern territory was called "Israel," while the southern section received the name of its principal tribe, "Judah." Isaiah refers to the "remnant of the house of Israel," because it had already been partially occupied by foreign invaders. Judah also felt threatened by the proximity of foreign armies. Isaiah wishes, therefore, to comfort and console this divided nation by reminding them that God, who called them into being, has not forgotten his beloved "child."

One of the most common experiences of those of us who are growing older is the sense that we are being forgotten, perhaps even ignored. The younger generation is taking over, which is inevitable, but we wonder whether these youngsters have completely forgotten all the contributions that we have made to make their world a better place in which to live and grow. Moreover, when our physical and psychic powers begin to falter, we may very well wonder whether God has forgotten us.

Therefore, the prophet Isaiah addresses us as well as the people of Israel. He uses maternal images to reassure us that God has not forgotten that we are his children. Indeed, God is pictured as our mother, who has carried us in her womb, and who can no more forget us than a mother can forget the child which she has nurtured in the most intimate way during those nine months of vital, life-sharing union.

God, we are told, has carried us, just as a mother carries her child, first in the womb, and then in her arms. And, most important of all, God cannot forget us, even though we grow ever more independent. We may indeed forget God in the days when we feel strong and seem to be free to live as we like. But God does not forget and, when we find that we are not as strong and free as we thought, God will be there, just as truly as ever.

How consoling are those words that Isaiah relays to us from our Creator: "Even to your old age I am he, even when you turn gray, I will carry you." We may feel that God has disappeared, but God has not forgotten. And it is especially in these latter days, when our earlier ambitions have been chastened by the reality of our mortal condition, that God's fierce attention to his beloved children is revealed.

It is true, of course, that we may not sense that fierce attention at first. But we must stir up our faith and trust the inspired message of the great prophet, Isaiah. In fact, we should read his words, over and over again, until they begin to penetrate our defenses against disappointment and touch that vulnerable place deep inside us where God's presence can be felt and our fears can be taken away. If we welcome these blessed words, their power will gradually convert our ways of thinking and bring about the conviction that they are meant to convey.

Human parents can sometimes be careless about the rearing of their children. But that can never be true of God. He can never disown those whom he has created, and he can never fail to "bear" them by his constant solicitude. When they are unable to walk on their own, he will "carry" them, and finally he will "save" them by offering all the help they will ever need to reach that goal of eternal life and happiness.

Because it is so difficult for us to believe that the all-powerful God could possibly be that concerned about us, Isaiah gives us God's words of reassurance: "I have spoken, and I will bring it to pass; I have planned, and I will do it." God does not speak lightly; his words are trustworthy beyond compare.

We recall how Isaiah gives us firm assurance in a later chapter: "For as the rain and the snow come down from heaven… giving seed to the sower and bread to the eater, so shall my word be that goes out from my mouth; it shall not return to me empty, but it shall accomplish that which I purpose, and succeed in the thing for which I sent it" (55:10-11). Comforting words indeed for those of us who may at times feel forgotten.

39

REJOICING IN THE LORD

Be careful then how you live, not as unwise people but as wise, making the most of the time, because the days are evil. So do not be foolish, but understand what the will of the Lord is. Do not get drunk with wine, for that is debauchery; but be filled with the Spirit, as you sing psalms and hymns and spiritual songs among yourselves, singing and making melody to the Lord in your hearts, giving thanks to God the Father at all times and for everything in the name of our Lord Jesus Christ (Eph 5:15-20).

We all hope that, when we have reached our later years, we will be able to look back and know that we have made a difference. Just to have survived is hardly enough. In the language of this passage, we will want to be able to say that we have lived wisely. This means that we have tried to understand what the opportunity of life is all about, especially as this is revealed by God, the Creator of all things. According to the Bible, the wise are those who have discovered God's purposes in their lives. They have learned from the Creator the place that each person has in the divine scheme of things.

We need to live wisely because, as St. Paul tells us, "the days are evil." This does not mean that there is some evil force that is taking control of the world and that we are helpless to resist it. This may seem to be the case at times, but St. Paul is actually referring to our tendency toward evil and darkness unless we freely and deliberately decide to choose goodness and light. Where there is no conscious choosing, there will be a victory of darkness. This means that we must be constantly concerned about "what the will of the Lord is."

St. Paul then tells us what the will of the Lord is not. It is not that pursuit of selfish pleasure that he calls "debauchery." This is a general term that includes all those many ways in which we are tempted to follow our baser instincts. St. Paul lists one of the principal examples of this when he warns us against getting "drunk with wine." From that example, we can easily deduce the many other ways in which we let ourselves overindulge in those things that are unworthy of God's children.

The only way in which we can resist and overcome the pull of selfishness in our lives is to be "filled with the Spirit." For St. Paul, the Spirit is that divine Person who dwells deep inside us and has the ability to convince us of God's love for us and of our certain victory if we stay close to Jesus. This role of the Spirit is clearly expressed by St. Paul in his Letter to the Galatians: "God has sent the Spirit of his Son into our hearts, crying, 'Abba! Father!' So you are no longer a slave but a child, and if a child then also an heir, through God" (4:6-7). There is no greater blessing in our lives than to know God as our loving Father and thus to be free of fear and certain of forgiveness.

The sure sign of this experience of God's Spirit in us is the joy that finds expression in song: "as you sing psalms and hymns and spiritual songs among yourselves, singing and making melody to the Lord in your hearts." We note that this joy is not some private experience but that it is shared with the whole community. Authentic Christian joy is always a joy that wants to be shared because it comes from a love that reaches out to others.

We hear a great deal today about the temptation to resort to drugs in order to achieve release from pain or to achieve a "high" of euphoria and pleasure. Life can indeed be boring and there is a kind of dull pain that permeates a life that seems to have no meaning. We all need to find a meaning in life that is satisfying and enjoyable. For St. Paul, this "high" is found, not in drugs or alcohol or over-medication with their inevitable letdown, but rather in the Spirit of God who wants to dwell in us and to liberate us from anxiety and boredom.

As we grow older, we become vulnerable to dependence on drugs in order to cope with life's problems. But we should know that there is a far better way to deal with sadness or fear. In the Spirit, and in the sharing of our faith, we can find a happiness that is so much more satisfying. Our singing voices may not be as strong as in our youth but the song in our hearts is the best possible medicine for whatever ails us.

Finally, St. Paul urges us to give "thanks to God the Father at all times and for everything in the name of our Lord Jesus Christ." To be a grateful human being is the final victory of God's gift of faith in us. And as we give thanks, we find more and more things to be grateful for…a sure recipe for happiness!

40

THE BEAUTY OF EXTRAVAGANT LOVE

As (Jesus)... sat at the table, a woman came with an ala-baster jar of very costly ointment of nard, and she broke open the jar and poured the ointment on his head. But some were there who said to one another in anger, "Why was the ointment wasted in this way? For this ointment could have been sold for more than three hundred denarii, and the money given to the poor." And they scolded her. But Jesus said, "Let her alone; why do you trouble her? She has performed a good service for me.... She has anointed my body beforehand for its burial. Truly I tell you, wherever the good news is proclaimed in the whole world, what she has done will be told in remembrance of her" (Mark 14:3-6, 8-9).

This little story of the anointing of Jesus by an anonymous woman occurs at the beginning of Mark's passion story and it seems to interrupt the flow of that narrative. For this reason, I was tempted one year to eliminate it from the material I was explaining in class since I was running short of time. But then I read the final verse in this passage, which tells us that what happened here must be told wherever in the whole world the gospel is proclaimed. With that reminder, I immediately restored it to my syllabus. But then I really began to wonder why this little story should be declared indispensable to the "greatest story ever told," namely, the passion, death and resurrection of Jesus.

Certain elements of this story seem to be exaggerated in order to make a point. The woman does not even wait to pull out the stopper of her precious cruet of ointment but actually breaks off the top, as if she cannot wait to use this ointment now that the long-awaited moment has arrived. Then she pours all of it on the head of Jesus. We are not told how much ointment was in the jar but it surely was far more than the few drops that would have been enough for a normal anointing.

The reaction of the bystanders also seems a bit exaggerated. We are told that they became angry and that they scolded her for being so wasteful. They immediately calculate the value of the ointment at 300 denarii, which would be about 300 days' wages—a tidy sum by anyone's assessment. Their grumbling and complaining about her foolishness and extravagance is in sharp contrast to what Jesus thinks about her action.

"But Jesus said, 'Let her alone; why do you trouble her? She has performed a good service for me.'" The Greek text can also be translated, "She has done a beautiful thing for me." And then he specifies exactly why his judgment is so different from that of the bystanders: "She has done what she could; she has anointed my body beforehand for its burial." The clear implication is that Jesus knows that his end is near and that he is naturally anxious about that. This sensitive woman is the only one there who has noticed this. She feels such compassion for Jesus that she does what she can for him. As it turns out, she is anticipating his death by performing the final, loving service of anointing his body.

I am convinced that this beautiful little story about the sensitivity of love is said to be indispensable for the passion story itself because it is in fact a miniature version of that story and is meant to help us understand what is at issue in the dying of Jesus. It serves a function similar to that of a key signature at the beginning of a piece of music, for it tells us how to read the "music" of the ultimate story which is the dying and rising of Jesus. This tells us then that Jesus will soon "break" the precious cruet that is his body and pour out the precious ointment that is his blood on all of us who are about to die!

When Jesus thus gives his life for us, he is showing that the passion story is far more about his loving than it is about his suffering. His loving and self-giving cause his suffering but it is his loving that saves the world. Moreover, what Jesus does will be called foolish and wasteful by many who cannot trust the power of unselfish love. And, perhaps more significantly, those followers of Jesus who do their best to imitate his love will also be called foolish and wasteful. But God knows the truth, that both Jesus and they are doing a "beautiful thing,"—in fact, the most beautiful thing that anyone could imagine.

This story challenges all Christians, but it speaks especially to those of us who are growing older. We need to know how necessary and how beautiful it is to "anoint" others with our loving concern. We may not be able to work as we once did, but we can still love and care…and that is the ultimate wisdom.

41

JESUS REVEALS THE FATHER'S LOVE FOR US

Pilate asked (Jesus), "So you are a king?" Jesus answered, "You say that I am a king. For this I was born, and for this I came into the world, to testify to the truth. Everyone who belongs to the truth listens to my voice" (John 18:37).

After teaching a course on John's Gospel for forty years or so, I have concluded that this verse is perhaps the most important passage in that entire gospel. This exchange between Jesus and Pilate is the climax of their discussion about the status of Jesus. Is he a king who will challenge the rule of Pilate? If so, why would the Jewish authorities bring him to Pilate, for it is clear that they would very much like to have their own king rather than this representative of the Roman Empire? It takes Pilate less than a minute to conclude that Jesus is no political threat to him.

Nonetheless, Pilate is very much interested in what kind of power Jesus may in fact possess. And so, when he asks Jesus whether he is a king, he is really asking whether he has another kind of power. When Jesus tells Pilate, "You say that I am a king," he is not just reminding Pilate of some earlier statement, for in fact Pilate has not said that at all. Rather, he is acknowledging that Pilate has brought up the question of power and he is therefore prepared to deal with that issue.

The statement of Jesus about his own kind of power is very solemn and very profound; in fact, it sums up the whole purpose of his presence in this world: "For this I was born, and for this I came into the world, to testify to the truth." He is saying that the eternal Word has taken on our human nature and has lived among us solely in order that he might have the opportunity to "testify to the truth." But this terse statement needs to be "unpacked." The meaning of these crucial words depends entirely upon the meaning of "truth" in John's gospel.

When John uses the word, "truth," he does not mean what we usually understand by this word, namely, philosophical or scientific truth. Rather, he means the truth that he has brought from his heavenly Father about the meaning and purpose of our human existence. It is nothing less than the revelation of God's purpose in creating us and putting us in this world. There is no other truth or revelation that could possibly be as important for us to understand. For if we do not understand why we are here, we cannot possibly know how we should live and what we can hope for.

The first and most important element in this revelation is the truth about God's love for us. Jesus not only told us this when he said, "God so loved the world that he gave his only Son" (John 3:16); he also proved this beyond any shadow of a doubt when he freely gave his life for us. "No one has greater love than this, to lay down one's life for one's friends" (John 15:13). When things don't go well, we have a hard time believing this but that is only because we still do not see the whole picture. In the meantime, it is the single most important reality in our lives.

God loves us in all kinds of mysterious ways, not only by making us feel loved, but also through loving family, dear friends, the beauty of nature, and in a thousand other ways. And as we count our many blessings, we become more and more aware of this gentle, tender love of the God who made us and who very much wants us to be happy with him forever.

As we are more and more affirmed by love, we become more free and more confident and more able to offer our love to others. This is not the romantic love that is celebrated in most songs and which certainly adds some spice to life. Rather, it is the unselfish love that causes us to reach out in loving service to all those who need our help. We are responsible for this kind of love only to the extent that we are free, but it is a solemn responsibility to the extent that we are in fact free.

The "truth" that Jesus brings to us is, therefore, this revelation about how to acquire freedom and then how to transform it into loving service. When he continues and says to Pilate, "Everyone who belongs to the truth listens to my voice," he is reminding us that we will be members of his flock only to the extent that we live the truth that he has given us.

As we grow older, we have more time to think about the purpose and outcome of our lives here on earth. Jesus is more than ready to "testify" to the truth in our own lives. We need to ask him to enlighten us about the love of his Father for us and about the hope that is based on that love. As we become more attuned to God's ways, we will also be able to bear witness to this goodness of God as we await the certain victory of this love when all is said and done.

42

THE ESSENCE OF THE GOSPEL

For I handed on to you as of first importance what I in turn had received: that Christ died for our sins in accordance with the scriptures, and that he was buried, and that he was raised on the third day in accordance with the scriptures, and that he appeared to Cephas, then to the twelve (1 Cor 15:3-5).

Paul wrote his First Letter to the Corinthians about 55 AD, which was before any gospel had been completed. This passage represents, therefore, the earliest and most succinct account of the passion, death and resurrection of Jesus. And since this climax of the earthly mission of Jesus is the high point of New Testament revelation, we have here four brief statements that summarize all of Christian revelation.

As we might expect, this summary statement is very carefully constructed. The first and third statements concern the death and resurrection of Jesus and are, therefore, the primary elements in this summary. The second and fourth statements are subordinate consequences of the two primary statements.

We should note, first of all, that Paul is reminding the Corinthians that he is passing on to them the ancient doctrine that he himself had received. This attests to the antiquity and trust-worthiness of this summary of gospel revelation. It tells us how the earliest proclamation of the meaning of the life and death of Jesus had been expressed. As such, its importance for us is unparalleled.

The first statement, "that Christ died for our sins," deserves our special attention. We note that Paul does not say that Jesus died; rather, it is Christ, i.e. the Messiah, the embodiment of all of Israel's hopes, who has expired. With the death of Jesus, all the hopes of the disciples seemed to have vanished as well. They were looking for a new King David, but Jesus died for a far nobler purpose, namely, to liberate us from the bondage of sin. Paul asserts that all this was in accordance with the scrip-tures, i.e. the Old Testament promises that God would eventu-ally liberate us through a definitive Exodus. (These "scriptures" can only be the Old Testament because what we know as the New Testament did not yet exist!)

This unexpected and seemingly tragic dying of the Messiah finds an echo in our own lives when our cherished plans are not fulfilled and when we have to deal with the pain of disappoint-ment. There are certainly many occasions when we must walk with those two disciples on the road to Emmaus and say, as they did, "we had hoped that he was the one to redeem Israel" (Luke 24:21). Or, in our case, we had hoped that such and such a plan or dream would be realized. Needless to say, as we grow older we have many more of these "disappointments" to remember.

The subordinate statement, "and that he was buried," seems at first glance to be irrelevant. But then we realize that not every-one was willing to accept the terrible news of the death of the Messiah. They continued to live in denial. But those few who did accept this unwelcome reality showed this by "burying" their Messiah, i.e. by accepting God's way of doing things. After all, we bury people only when we agree that they have died!

This has tremendous implications for our own lives. There are many times when we find it almost impossible to accept disappointments or losses. We may even blame God for this and give up religion altogether. At these times we should remember that our loss is hardly worse than the death of Jesus for his followers. This was simply not supposed to happen. Nonetheless, some of them sadly accepted this reality and believed that in the end God knows what he is doing.

The wisdom of their trust in God was then validated in the most dramatic manner: "and that he was raised on the third day." The loving self-sacrifice of Jesus led to a victory that was far more than the disciples dared dream, for they not only know now that Jesus is truly God's Messiah but, infinitely more than that, that he is God incarnate—that he is the Lord! His appearance to those faithful disciples—to Cephas (Peter) and the other apostles—is proof of this incredible victory of God's plan over their own plans and hopes (and ours too).

None of us really hopes or plans to grow old or become ill or eventually die. But we know that this is part of God's plan for us. This may make us wonder whether God really does love us. But we, like those first disciples, should rely on our faith in God's goodness as we trust implicitly that God will bring dramatic victory and new life…in his own gracious and loving way.

43

TRUSTING GOD IS A BEAUTIFUL GIFT

For to me, living is Christ and dying is gain. If I am to live in the flesh, that means fruitful labor for me; and I do not know which I prefer. I am hard pressed between the two: my desire is to depart and be with Christ, for that is far better; but to remain in the flesh is more necessary for you (Phil 1:21-24).

We know that Paul had special feelings for the Christians of Philippi. They seem to have responded with special generosity to his preaching , and he gladly reciprocated their devotion. It is not surprising, therefore, that Paul should bare his soul to these trustworthy friends. What he says to them has special meaning for us as well.

We can easily identify with Paul when he says that he is caught in a bind between living and dying. Not that we think every day about dying but, as we grow older, we are far more aware than we used to be that dying is an inevitable part of human life. I doubt that most of us would be ready to say, as Paul does, that "dying is gain." And the fairly obvious reason for this is that we are not able to say with Paul that for us "living is Christ." He sees death as the time when he will be finally united with the one who is the center of his life and who is more precious to him than anyone or anything else could ever be.

I don't think we should react to this by saying, Well, Paul was a saint and I don't have much chance of sharing his experience. It is true that we may not have the spiritual maturity of Paul, but we can certainly strive to move in that direction. Christ wants to be our friend just as much as he wanted to be the friend of Paul! We were made to be one with him and, given half a chance, every fiber of our being would eagerly respond to his presence.

The major problem that we have in our relationship with Jesus is our incredible tendency to be distracted. We live in a world that is so full of images and sounds that are designed to attract and hold our attention that, unless we make a conscious effort to resist, they will so mesmerize us that we will never see what is really important in life. The solution is to beg God for the first, sweet taste of that banquet that the experience of Christ in our lives can be. Hopefully, this will wean us away from our addiction to the "junk food" on which many of us try to survive.

We can only be filled with admiration at Paul's positive attitude about his choices in life. To live on a while longer is good because it will allow him to continue to help others whom he loves. But to die is good too because that will allow him to be fully united with Christ who is the love of his life. What a contrast that is with the way we often see our choices. We may be tired of this life which has become painful and tiresome, but we also fear the next life because it is unknown and threatening.

The solution to this dilemma is to find a closer relationship with Jesus. Then the long, empty hours of old age will be filled with the enjoyment of his presence. But if the end seems near, that will be no major problem either, because we will then enter into the fullness of our union with Jesus. To the extent, therefore, that we come to know and love the Lord we will also reach that happy dilemma that Paul experienced.

There is much talk these days about the pros and cons of assisted suicide. In a secular society, where the only meaning in life is between birth and death, it makes a lot of sense to arrange one's exit from this world when life is no longer enjoyable. But for those of us who believe that this present life is only the preparation for another far more meaningful life, there should be no question about the need to allow God to decide when we make that transition. It is simply a matter of trusting the goodness of God.

In this regard, the message of Paul is also quite clear: "but to remain in the flesh is more necessary for you." His sole concern is not his own escape from suffering but the benefit that his suffering may provide for those whom he loves. We can never know at the moment how much others may benefit from our own patient endurance when life is no longer enjoyable. Nor can we know how much good this patience and trust can do for us too.

In many ways, the most beautiful gift that we can give to another person is the gift of trust. And the same is true in our relationship with God. How fitting it is that we should have this golden opportunity as the last decision of our lives on this earth!

44

ALWAYS AWARE
OF GOD'S PRESENCE

Hear, O Israel: The LORD *is our God, the* LORD *alone. You
shall love the* LORD *your God with all your heart, and with all
your soul, and with all your might. Keep these words that I am
commanding you today in your heart. Recite them to your children and talk about them when you are at home and when you
are away, when you lie down and when you rise. Bind them as
a sign on your hand, fix them as an emblem on your forehead,
and write them on the doorposts of your house and on your
gates.* (Deut 6:4-9).

This is one of the truly golden texts of the Old Testament and
it is rightly called Israel's profession of faith. Its full import can
be understood, however, only if we realize that the word translated as "LORD" is really the personal name of Israel's God, that
is, "Yahweh." We find this name strange and most translations
try to avoid it but it is God's personal name, whereas "LORD" is
the name of God's "office".

When I was rector of our seminary, I did not mind if the seminarians called me "Fr. Rector." However, I wanted to be known
to my confreres as "Demetrius." Otherwise, who am I when I

cease to be the Rector? "LORD," like Rector, is the name of an office; Yahweh and Demetrius are personal names. This secret, personal name of God was revealed to Moses and implied profound trust and intimacy. One's personal name is like an unlisted telephone number, which is never given to strangers. We know that when that number rings it is a friend calling, one who would not disturb us without good cause.

With this in mind, we note immediately the difference between "The LORD is our God" and "Yahweh is our God." The name "Yahweh" derives from the Hebrew word "to be" and the implication is that the God of Israel is the only one who truly exists and who is the creator of all things. Most of all, however, the Israelites remember that this God took pity on them in their Egyptian bondage and loved them and made them his own people. No wonder then that they are commanded to "love the LORD your God with all your heart and with all your soul, and with all your might."

The remainder of the quotation is a series of recommendations for expressing Israel's wholehearted devotion to the God who has been so good to them. This should be the primary content of the education that they pass on to their children; they are to make God's reality and presence so real in their lives that all their familiar activities are to be influenced by that consciousness. The author even goes so far as to suggest practical means by which they will be reminded of God's presence. We are not altogether certain about the meaning of these suggestions, but they obviously have the same intent that is expressed when we say that we will tie a string around a finger to be sure to remember some important task or meeting or date.

This text summons all of us to get our priorities in order. Not only should God hold a primary place of honor in our attention but we soon learn that, if our relationship with God is neglected, we will quickly find it difficult to relate to other persons in a healthy way. Those who earnestly entertain the presence of God will feel so affirmed that they will not be so desperate for human affirmation. This will enable them to respond in a free and realistic way to the free offer of love from others. Sadly but truly, those who seek love desperately are the very ones who frighten people away with their obsessive behavior.

At first glance, it may seem that being so aware of God's presence may be itself a distraction that could interfere with our attention to the task at hand. However, it has been my experience that not all distractions are bad. Some are benign distractions which actually enable us to be more focused on what we are doing. Thus, for example, if a mother who is preparing dinner at a hot stove and glances momentarily at her child playing on the kitchen floor, smiling with love, she is not thereby more apt to be burned or scalded. Her loving glance, unlike an angry thought, enables her to be more present to the reality of her work.

In a similar manner, the benign distraction of those who are conscious of God's love for them will actually enhance their ability to do their work with full attention and in a more efficient way. For example, a person who loves and feels loved is a much safer driver than one who is angry or frustrated.

This benign distraction is reinforced by regular intervals of prayer when our attention is directed completely to our loving Lord. At other times, God will never be far from our thoughts and can be easily recalled at a moment's notice. This is the secret for becoming calm and confident in every circumstance of life, but especially when we grow older.

45

BEING TRANSFIGURED BY THE MESSAGE OF JESUS

Now about eight days after these sayings Jesus took with him Peter and John and James, and went up on the mountain to pray. And while he was praying, the appearance of his face changed, and his clothes became dazzling white. Suddenly they saw two men, Moses and Elijah, talking to him. They appeared in glory and were speaking of his departure, which he was about to accomplish at Jerusalem.... Then from the cloud came a voice that said, "This is my Son, my Chosen; listen to him!" (Luke 9:28-31, 35).

We all recognize this passage as Luke's version of the Transfiguration. It is surprising to see how Luke introduces this story by referring to a previous event. Gospel stories are usually separate accounts without any temporal references. When we examine this unusual reference, we discover that he is referring to what happened at Caesarea Philippi where Jesus asked his disciples about his identity, first among the general public, and then among themselves. This is followed by the first prediction of his passion: "The Son of Man must undergo great suffering..." (Luke 9:22).

This unexpected announcement from one whose miraculous power seemed invincible stunned the disciples. It also marked a dramatic turning point in the mission of Jesus. The Galilean ministry with its miracles and apparent promises of an earthly, political Messiah is ending and the Judean period will now begin and lead to Jesus' death and resurrection. The Transfiguration thus takes on special importance, not only for Jesus but for us also, for we too must make the journey that he made. The gospels suggest as much when they give no name to this mountain. In fact, we must all visit this height before we die...and we cannot all visit the Holy Land.

Jesus did not climb this mountain in order to have a better view of the countryside. Luke tells us that he went there to pray and notes that something special happened to him "while he was praying." We can well imagine that he is in communion with his heavenly Father, as was his custom, in order to receive reassurance about this sudden turn in his journey toward Jerusalem and his ordeal there. After all, it was this heavenly Father who had called him at his baptism, "my Son, the Beloved" (Luke 3:22). In our own experience, this would be like our turning to God in prayer after learning that we are suddenly in a life-threatening situation.

At this moment, an aura of light surrounds Jesus. His face and his clothing glow with the intensity of this light. What is happening here? I do not think that the Father is focusing a light on Jesus just to reassure his disciples. After all, only three of them were there, and there is no evidence that they were reassured. Rather, he is leading Jesus to a profound and ecstatic realization that his mission to save others is to be accomplished, not by warfare and violence (as we humans might imagine), but rather in the divine way of loving and caring...and therefore suffering and dying... and therefore rising to new life!

Jesus literally glows as this incredible divine way of saving the world dawns upon him. (I have sometimes seen a little transfiguration of this kind on the faces of my better students as they suddenly grasp the meaning of something that I have been trying to explain to them!) This means that Jesus actually grew in his awareness of what his mission would require of him, just as we do.

Moses and Elijah are there, first of all to signal to us the supreme importance of this experience of Jesus, but also because they too had met God on a mountaintop and had learned in ecstasy how they were to carry out their own vocations. When Moses came down from Mt. Sinai, his face shone so brightly that the Israelites could not look at him (Exod 34:30). And it was on Mt. Horeb (another name for Mt. Sinai) that Elijah heard the powerful voice of God in "sheer silence" (1 Kgs 19:12).

Then comes the wonderful and unconditional reassurance of the heavenly Father as Jesus hears the same words that he had heard at his baptism, "This is my Son, my Chosen," but something new and very important is added, "Listen to him" (Luke 9:35). In other words, now that Jesus has discovered the ultimate secret of God's plan for him, he is prepared, as never before, to teach us how to live and love and die and rise with him!

As we approach our later years, we too need to meet God in a new way and learn that the most important thing that we can discover in life is how to love unselfishly, and how to die in many little ways for the sake of others, and how thereby to be ready for our own resurrection with Jesus. The "Galilean" period of our lives, with all its little victories and joys, must now give way to a deeper wisdom about loving and caring and forgiving and praying. In this way, our later years can be more fruitful and satisfying than anything that happened before, as we "listen to him," and find that our faces glow with the wonderful good news about the real purpose of our lives.

46

PRAYING TO A LOVING FATHER

"Pray then in this way: Our Father in heaven, hallowed be your name. Your kingdom come. Your will be done, on earth as it is in heaven" (Matt 6:9-10).

In the journey of faith, prayer is like the oxygen needed for an Olympic runner. When we reach a certain age we can identify especially with the long-distance runner. Sprinting is no longer an option. What we need is the strength to make it through each day. On the spiritual plane, this means that we need the oxygen of frequent prayer. Fortunately, time for prayer is usually also readily available. Such time is precious and should never be squandered on such things as watching TV or just worrying.

There are a thousand and one kinds of prayer and most of them are helpful. But there is only one prayer that has been given to us by Jesus himself. This "Lord's Prayer" is, therefore, in a class by itself. It is, in fact, the only truly indispensable prayer for us Christians. Every word needs to be savored and caressed with tender love and trust. St. Teresa of Avila is supposed to have said that the best way to be a contemplative person is simply to say the "Our Father," but to do so very, very slowly.

The word, "Father," is a human word, which can be applied to God only in a partially accurate way. Its masculine connotation is irrelevant since God possesses the fullness of both genders. What is appropriately applied to God are the strength and goodness that are the attributes of a good human father. As a loving parent, therefore, God offers us both tender concern and incredible power. He also guarantees for his good children a rich inheritance of happiness and peace.

This divinely loving parent is said to be "our" father because, to the extent that we experience his loving concern, we can afford to put aside that destructive competition that exists between children who are starved for parental love and attention. Thus, this gracious Father is not "my" father but a Father who is gladly shared with others in the community of faith.

Moreover, he is said to be "in heaven," not as if in some distant abode far above us, but because he awaits us with open arms in our true homeland at the end of time. Thus, as we learn to trust this divinely parental love, we will feel drawn, as if by some powerful magnetic attraction, to that wonderful inheritance reserved for us by our heavenly Father.

Jesus then asks us to make three petitions that concern our relationship to this heavenly Father. In the original Greek, these requests are in the aorist imperative tense. This means that we are asking for final and definitive action in three distinct dimensions of our relationship with God. When I was a student in Jerusalem, my professor illustrated the special nature of this Greek tense by clapping his hands sharply and saying, "There; that is the aorist tense!" It signifies an action that happens definitively, once and for all.

We may be surprised to learn therefore that, when we pray that God's name be hallowed, we are actually asking for the coming of the end of the world! For it is only at the end of time that God's good name or reputation will be restored after he has been blamed for everything from personal sin to natural disaster. We dare to pray for an end that seems frightening to us because we have learned hopefully to trust the love and goodness of our heavenly Father.

We also pray that God's kingdom come, and again, once and for all. We are not asking that God's power be unleashed to put in their places those whom we do not like. Rather, we ask for the fulfillment of God's dream for his beloved children. This too will happen only at the end of time and, as we come to experience more and more the love of God, we will indeed be impelled to pray for that wonderful day when God's love will be victorious over all our failings and fears.

Finally, we pray that God's "will" be done everywhere in the universe. This will of God, like his kingdom, refers to his loving plan for us. We often think that we know better than God how the world should be run. But, as we learn to trust God's love, we will also be able to let him continue to "write straight with crooked lines." Since trust is one of the most precious fruits of real love, we will gradually learn to trust God, through thick and thin, as we come to know and love him—and as we pray this best of all Christian prayers.

47

PROVIDING FOR OUR SPIRITUAL JOURNEY

Give us this day our daily bread. And forgive us our debts, as we also have forgiven our debtors. And do not bring us to the time of trial, but rescue us from the evil one (Matt 6:11-13).

In the first half of the "Our Father" we express our trust in God's goodness as we pray for the realization of God's wonderful designs at the end of time. Now we turn to consideration of our own needs as we try to make our way to that blessed homecoming. We ask our heavenly Father, therefore, for what we need as we make our journey of faith. These petitions are especially urgent for those of us who have grown older because the last stage of the journey is always the most difficult.

When we ask God to give us each day "our daily bread," we are asking for that nourishment which is most necessary for those who are on a long and difficult journey, that is, the gift of hope. When we lose hope of completing a journey successfully, we have no option except to stop and turn back. In the case of a spiritual journey, that means to turn one's back on the future and to begin to live in the barren land of a past that is dead and gone.

So We Do Not Lose Heart

This was the great temptation of Israel in the Sinai desert as they pleaded with Moses to take them back to Egypt. The familiar but fatal past seemed more attractive to them than the unknown and ominous future. And so we ask our heavenly Father for the precious gift that enables us to see the future as an illuminated horizon where we will find the exquisite joy of a child who runs with joy into the arms of a loving parent.

There is another obstacle for those who make the journey of faith and it is something that every traveler will recognize. Those of us who have made a lengthy journey have inevitably been confronted with the problem of how much baggage we can afford to take along. We want to prepare for all possible needs but we also must be aware that excessive baggage can be an encumbrance that can easily spoil the enjoyment of our journey. Just managing the baggage can interfere with the care-free nature of our trip.

In the case of the most important journey of our lives—the one that will take us hopefully to our heavenly home—the baggage that can load us down and can take the joy out of this adventure is the heavy baggage of guilt. One does not have to live very long before one acquires that heavy load of concern about past failings and mistakes. We remember and often dwell upon those times when we did things which have hurt others, sometimes severely, or the times when we failed to do or say something when it would have made all the difference. We tell ourselves that we should not weep over spilled milk but that does not prevent us from feeling badly about what might have been.

And so we ask our loving Father to make us understand that we are forgiven for these past failings, for which we are truly sorry, so that we can unload the baggage of guilt and regret that weighs us down. For we want to be able to run and skip on this journey with wings on our heels and joy in our hearts.

And then we make a solemn pledge to do all we can to help our fellow travelers to know that they too are forgiven for past failings. This means giving up old grudges and hurts that can simply magnify the pain that we may have felt. We realize how serious this matter is when we read the words that follow the Our Father in the gospel: "For if you forgive others their trespasses, your heavenly Father will also forgive you; but if you do not forgive others, neither will you Father forgive your trespasses" (Matt 6:14-15).

Forgiving is one of the most difficult things that we face in our lives. This does not mean that we are required to forget past hurts. That may well be impossible. But it does mean that we must let go of the resentment that we may feel toward someone who has injured or betrayed us. The Holy Spirit will help us to do this, for Jesus told his disciples after the resurrection: "Receive the Holy Spirit. If you forgive the sins of any, they are forgiven them; if you retain the sins of any, they are retained" (John 20:22-23). This represents a terrible responsibility but also a glorious opportunity. We must be very careful not to let it pass.

Finally, we ask God to be with us at the end of our lives and to protect us from the assaults of our old enemy, the devil. He will want to frighten us by suggesting that God cannot forgive us, or that there is no light beyond the darkness of death. It is immensely consoling to be able to say to God: Your Son, Jesus, told us to remind you to be with us with your love and forgiveness when the end comes. How could this loving Father fail to respond to what his own beloved Son has asked for us?

48

BEING GLAD ALL OUR DAYS

The days of our life are seventy years, or perhaps eighty, if we are strong; even then their span is only toil and trouble; they are soon gone and we fly away…. Satisfy us in the morning with your steadfast love, so that we may rejoice and be glad all our days (Ps 90:10, 14).

The Bible is very realistic about our situation as fragile human beings. Even so, when the psalmist says that we may live to seventy or, in rare instances, even to eighty, he is being very optimistic for those days. This doesn't mean that seventy or eighty was the life expectancy in ancient Israel; it means simply that, if you made it to adulthood, you had a reasonable chance to reach such an old age.

We must note, however, that the psalmist adds immediately that such old men and women can expect to experience "toil and trouble," which is really a significant understatement. In the days when proper eye care was non-existent, old age almost always meant blindness. Nor was there any remedy for such things as appendicitis, arthritis or other common maladies. Even so, the days of life are precious and one cannot be pleased to see that "they are soon gone, and we fly away."

Thus far, the situation described is true of all human beings. Even when life is long, it seems too short! Without faith in God there is no recourse except to grin and bear it, or perhaps to end one's life by some unnatural means. The pessimism of pagan philosophy is dominant in such a situation. In the ancient epic of Gilgamesh, the barmaid told our hero who is desperately searching for immortality: "My friend, the gods have kept life for themselves. For us there is only one recourse: Eat, drink and be merry, for tomorrow you die." From this perspective, there is but a brief moment of youth and strength, after which there is only misery and death.

The psalmist rejects such a pessimistic assessment and declares instead that there is a good and loving God, who does not keep life for himself alone, but truly wishes to share his life with us. After a period of trial and testing, God offers us a life that knows no end. This is that new "morning"—that new beginning—to which the Psalmist refers when he says to God: "Satisfy us in the morning with your steadfast love, so that we may rejoice and be glad all our days."

The psalmist could not see so far ahead, but we now know that this "new morning" is the joyful Easter morning that followed the death of Jesus. If we follow him in a life of loving service, we too will see a wonderful new morning after this life with all its adversities and shadows. Our departure from this life is, therefore, not the real ending at all. It simply marks the beginning of a new life with Jesus in our true homeland. When that happens, we will know for the first time about the depth and power of God's "steadfast love" for us.

There are frequent references in the Psalms to this "steadfast love" of God for his chosen people. First of all, it refers to the love that they experienced when God took pity on them and led them out of the terrible bondage of Egypt. This unconditional love enabled them to overcome the sense of being helpless slaves as it gave them a confidence and an identity that made them a free and responsible people. Today we might say that they were delivered from the crippling bondage of low self-esteem. They could now dare to hope and plan for the future because they now understood that God wanted them to do more than make bricks.

This love of God is also called "steadfast" because it is not only generous beyond imagination but also entirely reliable. In other words, it is not like the love that we often experience, that is, a love that is intense for a while but then turns inconstant and unreliable. This is expressed very well in the plaintive question that we must ask when someone tells us how much he or she loves us: "Yes, but will you love me when I'm old and gray?" The psalmist reminds us that God will indeed love us when we are old and gray…in fact, more then than ever!

It is true that we cannot be convinced of God's steadfast love until our eyes of faith are opened and we begin to see as God sees. How do we arrive at such a blessed state? We must pray constantly for such a vision and be confident that God will give it to us if we are persistent and patient. We must also strive as much as possible to lead a life that is in keeping with God's call to live unselfishly. If we do this, we can be confident that, when the end comes, God will give us that wonderful assurance that a bright new day awaits us, so that, as the psalmist promises, "we may rejoice and be glad all our days."

49

THE LOVE OF JESUS IS STRONGER THAN DEATH

When they came to the house of the leader of the synagogue, (Jesus) saw a commotion, people weeping and wailing loudly. When he had entered, he said to them, "Why do you make a commotion and weep? The child is not dead but sleeping." And they laughed at him. Then he put them all outside, and took the child's father and mother and those who were with him, and went in where the child was. He took her by the hand and said to her, "Talitha, cum," which means, "Little girl, get up!" And immediately the girl got up and began to walk about (she was twelve years of age). At this they were overcome with amazement (Mark 5:38-42).

There are few stories in Mark's gospel that are more comforting for us mortals than this beautiful and simple story about Jesus raising to life a twelve year old girl. It was undoubtedly a special moment for the parents and friends of the little girl, but it also has profound symbolic meaning for all of us. We cannot fail to see the contrast between the mourners who have gathered to weep and wail and the confident intervention of Jesus. They have learned from experience about the power of death, which always seems to have the last word. But Jesus has come to change all that.

The bystanders are so sure that death cannot be overcome that they actually laugh at Jesus. Hidden behind them is the devil himself who mocks our hopes and tells us that this is the only life that we really have and that we had better make the most of it. We must not make the mistake of taking the claim of Satan lightly because everyone of us is profoundly influenced by the common assumption that we can't really count very much on a life beyond this one. Otherwise, why would we be so afraid to let go of the life we have?

It is surprising to hear Mark say that this little girl was exactly twelve years old. Is this fact really important for the story? I think it surely is, and that becomes clear when we reflect on the symbolic meaning of a twelve year old girl. Surely there is no more beautiful and inspiring symbol of life and hope than such a young girl, standing as she does on the threshold of fruitful adulthood. Someone told me once that the only way we can grasp the horror of nuclear holocaust is to try to imagine a world in which there would be no little girls!

We should also note that Mark has Jesus speak in his native language of Aramaic, a dialect of Hebrew. This is intended to emphasize the intimate and personal nature of Jesus' intervention to challenge the seemingly invincible power of death in our world. For Jesus, this is a deeply personal commitment to overcome death and to bring wonder and laughter into our world in place of the pervasive and seemingly inevitable refuge in wailing and despair.

The little girl that Jesus raised from the dead is, therefore, a dramatic symbol of our own precious hope for eternal life. She seems so fragile just as there is evidence all around us that we cannot cope with the power of physical decline and death. But Jesus contradicts this pessimistic assessment of our situation. He says, "No," to fearsome death and, "Yes," to fragile life, and he does so with such conviction that we can trust his promise unconditionally.

We see all this in the climax of Jesus' own life. When he was condemned to death and hung on the cross, it appeared that Satan and death had carried the day. We can scarcely imagine a more hopeless situation. But God said, "No," to his death and "Yes" to his life, and thus a risen Lord replaced the suffering and dying Jesus. God did this because Jesus loved in an unselfish and divine way, which is the secret of the victory of life over death.

We too, like the bystanders in the gospel, should be "overcome with amazement" as we witness this little "preview" of the resurrection. There is no doubt that we will feel the power of death and will be sorely tempted to think it is "all over." However, this simple gospel story tells us that we must also look for and be open to the much greater power of God's love, expressed in our midst through the loving presence of Jesus. This trust in God's love for us will dispel the darkness and send away the mourners.

As our trust grows stronger, the bright "little girl" of hope within us will prove to be much stronger than the dark bluster of death. Then we can await with confidence the command of Jesus to "rise up." Suddenly, the darkness will be dispelled and the resurrection dawn will announce the victory of God's love in our own lives.

50

BEING WISE AS WELL AS WEALTHY

And (Jesus) said to them, "Take care! Be on your guard against all kinds of greed; for one's life does not consist in the abundance of possessions." Then he told them a parable: "The land of a rich man produced abundantly. And he thought to himself, 'What should I do, for I have no place to store my crops?' Then he said, 'I will do this: I will pull down my barns and build larger ones, and there I will store all my grain and my goods. And I will say to my soul, 'Soul, you have ample goods laid up for many years; relax, eat, drink, be merry.' But God said to him, 'You fool! This very night your life is being demanded of you. And the things you have prepared, whose will they be?' So it is with those who store up treasures for themselves but are not rich toward God" (Luke 12:15-21).

Luke was born and raised in the prosperous Roman city of Antioch in Syria. Of all the evangelists, he seems to have understood best the dangers of material wealth for a follower of Christ. He had witnessed how miserably poor some were, while others lived in luxury. He also noticed that wealth tends to blind people to the spiritual dimension of human life. It has a subtle but very real drugging effect that makes people insensitive to the condition of others and which causes them to blame the poor for their own poverty. All this has the potential for personal tragedy as the inevitable judgment brings the terrible surprise of rejection by God.

Luke reflects on this situation in various places but one of his most telling stories is found in the parable of the rich farmer. It is not difficult to follow the story line: A farmer is blest with fertile land and soon discovers that his barns are not sufficient to store all the grain from his fields. Instead of thinking about sharing his bounty with others who are less fortunate, and perhaps even starving, he is concerned only with how he can keep all that he has acquired. For the rich invariably find that, no matter how much they have, it is never quite enough.

The self-centeredness of the rich farmer is most effectively expressed in the manner in which he deals with his "problem." He begins to talk to himself! I think this tells us so much about his outlook on life. Because he is rich, he assumes that he must also be wise—so wise in fact that he need not seek advice from anyone. After all, does his good fortune not prove that he is smarter than anyone else he knows? The simple fact is that success in various business enterprises may prove that one is intelligent or lucky but it is no proof at all that one is wise. For wisdom is not about how to run a railroad but about how to live a good life under God.

And so the rich farmer looks in the mirror (from which we rarely learn anything useful) and asks what he should do about his bountiful harvest. Not only does his voice come back predictably with the advice to build bigger barns but it also tells him to do what pagans have considered an ideal from the dawn of time: "relax, eat, drink, be merry." This is the advice given by the barmaid in the famous Babylonian Epic of Gilgamesh when this hero comes to her place and tells her that he is looking for immortality. "O Gilgamesh," she said, "the gods have kept life for themselves. For us it remains only to eat, drink and be merry, for tomorrow we die."

The pagan philosophy of selfishness makes sense only when one is young and strong and wealthy. It has nothing helpful to say to the very young and the very old and the poor ones of the earth. But it is precisely these, most of all, who are favored by God and loved by Jesus. No wonder then that God gives a chilling response to the self-advice of the rich farmer: "You fool! This very night your soul is being demanded of you. And the things you have prepared, whose will they be?" We must understand "You fool" in the sense of "You most unwise man," for what he is doing is the most stupid thing that one could imagine. He is dead wrong about how to live a successful life…and now it is too late to do anything about it.

Most of us who are in the so-called golden years of life are blest in so many ways. We may have acquired some wealth or we may be especially talented, or we may at least have a wonderful wealth of experience. We must at all cost avoid becoming so possessive that we do not want to share what we have with others. There is nothing more pitiful than a wealthy or talented old man or woman who has become crabby and self-centered and judgmental. Just as there is nothing so beautiful as an older person who gladly shares his or her wealth with all those younger folks who need wisdom and who are probably just about as undeserving as we ourselves once were!

51

SHARING OUR LIFE WITH JESUS

I am the true vine, and my Father is the vinegrower. He removes every branch in me that bears no fruit. Every branch that bears fruit he prunes to make it bear more fruit.... Abide in me as I abide in you. Just as the branch cannot bear fruit by itself unless it abides in the vine, neither can you unless you abide in me.... Those who abide in me and I in them bear much fruit (John 15:1-2, 4-5).

In order to appreciate fully the imagery used by Jesus in this passage, we must know something about viniculture or the cultivation of grapes. In a mature vineyard, the vinestock is a short, thick trunk with roots that reach deep into the soil where moisture can be found during the long summer months when in Palestine there is no rain. This endless sunshine is important for the sweetness of the grapes. From that trunk, branches or vines grow in great profusion. The health and productivity of these vines depends upon the sap that is produced by the vinestock.

This is a daring image when we realize that it is used by Jesus to describe the relationship that we must have with him and his heavenly Father. Not only is the the Bread and Wine to be consumed; he is now presented as one who shares the "sap," or vital fluid, of life with us. It is as if we are called to share his very life-blood! We can scarcely imagine a more personal and intimate analogy to describe our union with him.

This union is made possible by our faith, which puts us in touch with the reality of God in our world. God is indeed present and very much wants to be one with us, but we must trust the gift of faith which enables us to be so sure of the divine presence that our lives are profoundly transformed. When this happens, every breath we take is in harmony with him and every decision we make reflects the reality of his presence. When we are thus united with him, we extend his presence to others and become "fruitful." Conversely, if we are not united with him in our loving, we will be cut off of the vinestock as unfruitful branches.

This communion with God does not mean, however, that our lives will be free of suffering. That is why Jesus says that "Every branch that bears fruit he prunes to make it bear more fruit." Anyone who has attempted to grow grapes will soon learn how important it is to prune the vines. The reason is that the vinestock puts out far more numerous and longer branches than it can reasonably support. If the vines are not cut back, there will be many grape clusters, but the grapes will be small and sour and not suitable therefore for making wine.

In the analogy that Jesus uses, the "pruning" by his Father, the vinegrower, means the suffering that comes from living an unselfish and other-centered life. Jesus tells us that this is what the Father asks of us and he is also quite clear about the pain that this will bring. It is never easy to give up one's own preference for the sake of others. But this is what being one with Jesus means. It is also what being fruitful means. Instead of being constantly preoccupied with one's own problems, one takes note of the problems in the lives of others and is willing to reach out to them in love and service.

As we grow older, we become ever more conscious of our human frailty and there is a real danger that we will become so self-absorbed that we do not notice the condition of those around us. The challenge of Jesus is that we deliberately choose to look beyond ourselves and become truly interested in the welfare of others. Sometimes this means simply that we look at them and name them and ask ourselves, "What can I do to make his or her life more pleasant or more tolerable?" Gradually this will make us a blessing in the lives of others, rather than the burden that we can easily become.

I think there may be another way in which we can experience the pruning that will make us more fruitful. In our later years, we sometimes find it very difficult to trust the goodness of God. We may even wonder whether God really knows that we exist and really cares about us. But trust means that we recall the earlier goodness of God to us and, on that basis, choose to believe that God loves us, even if this is not apparent at the present time.

Children who have learned that their parents love them will be willing to do things that they don't understand simply because they trust the ones who have loved them and cared for them. We too have good reason to know that God has been good to us and it is a wonderful opportunity now for us to trust this God who really does love us more than we can imagine.

52

DISCOVERING GOD'S LOVING PRESENCE

In the day of my trouble I seek the LORD; in the night my hand is stretched out without wearying; my soul refuses to be comforted. I think of God, and I moan; I meditate, and my spirit faints. You keep my eyelids from closing; I am so troubled that I cannot speak.... I will call to mind the deeds of the LORD; I will remember your wonders of old.... With your strong arm you redeemed your people (Ps 77:2-4, 11, 15).

The Psalms are filled with praise for God, as well as thanksgiving for blessings received or favors anticipated. But there are also many and vivid expressions of distress and anguish about the miseries that beset our human condition. The Bible as a whole does not indulge in romantic or dreamy conceptions of life. The warts and wrinkles are all there, along with exquisite beauty and noble deeds. I have often noted that you can smell in the Old Testament the sheep and the garlic as well as the roses of Sharon!

The difference between our own experience of human suffering and that of the psalmist is that we often remain helpless and fearful, whereas such suffering prompts the psalmist to "seek the Lord." If we are getting along in years, we know very well what the psalmist means when he says that the dark hours of the night magnify our malaise so that our souls refuse to be comforted. Nothing seems to soothe our fears or relieve our anxiety.

Even thinking about God is not a magical remedy. Such thoughts do not keep one from the empty feeling of helplessness. It seems often that, just when we need most to feel the presence of God, there is no hint of his presence. There seems to be nothing left but the hollow echoes of our own voices. Feeling alone is a common experience at all stages of life, but never more so than in our later years.

Suddenly the mood changes, however. This happens, according to the psalmist, when we call to mind "the deeds of the Lord" and remember his "wonders of old." The clear implication is that God's presence is felt, not by thinking about a distant powerful One, but by recalling how God has acted in our human history. A real, but largely theoretical, divinity is now replaced by that divine One who has wielded his power and manifested his love in the lives of those who have gone before us. However, since God's acts occur in an eternal present, they are happening in our world also. If God cared so much for them he cares just as much for us.

Israel always thought of God as of one who has acted in history, notably at the time of the Exodus. The psalmist recalls that it was his own ancestors who had languished in slavery and who had been liberated and formed into a unique people with a special mission. And he recalls also that this happened primarily because this God had shown his love for them. His love for them existed long before his intervention to save them.

It was Moses, a real historical person, who had convinced

the Israelites of God's love for them. In some truly miraculous way, they were able to trust the words of Moses and to believe that there is One more powerful than the Pharaoh and, wonder of wonders, that he is also ever so kind and gentle and compassionate. The steely cold eyes of their taskmasters in Egypt are replaced with the soft, smiling eyes of their divine deliverer. This is history; this is not just wishful thinking!

This wonderful story had been told from one generation to the next, and it was told to the psalmist by his own parents. He had loved to hear this narrative and savored every detail of it. God has shown his love to his people and to himself...and God has chosen him to write about his goodness. What else could one ask for?

We too need to remember, not only the wonderful story of Exodus, but especially the story of the new Exodus when Jesus gave his life because he loved us and thus enabled us to be free from guilt and fear. More than any member of Israel, we should rejoice in this final, dramatic manifestation of God's love for us: "For God so loved the world that he gave his only Son, so that everyone who believes in him may not perish but may have eternal life" (John 3:16).

Every time we participate in the Eucharist we are put in touch with God's greatest act of love in our human history. For in this great sacrament we are invited to share in the very act by which God gave his only Son so that we might be free and hopeful and unafraid. There will never be a more perfect opportunity to say to God with the psalmist that we "remember your wonders of old." We know this because our parents told it to us; it is more trustworthy than any other word that we will ever hear!

53

JESUS SUFFERED BECAUSE HE LOVED

Then Pilate took Jesus and had him flogged. And the soldiers wove a crown of thorns and put it on his head, and they dressed him in a purple robe. They kept coming up to him, saying, "Hail, king of the Jews!" and striking him on the face... So Jesus came out, wearing the crown of thorns and the purple robe. Pilate said to them, "Here is the man!" (John 19:1-3, 5).

One of the features that separates the Bible from much of religious literature is its relentless realism. It does not tell us that God is an indulgent deity who doesn't really care whether we sin or not. And it doesn't tell us that the story of Jesus should be limited to his kind and gentle presence in Galilee. That is indeed a part of the story and it should not be ignored. However, the full and final revelation of Jesus came at the end of his earthly life in the story of his suffering, death and resurrection.

The account of the suffering of Jesus must not, however, be taken out of context. It does not mean that human suffering is a good thing in itself. But it does say in the clearest terms that there can be no real loving without suffering. The reason for that is quite simply that, when we truly care for others, we will inevitably have to put aside many of our own preferences in order to accommodate their needs. In some cases this may require a person to give up his life rather than to betray the truth which others need so desperately.

The suffering of Jesus in his passion was intense, but it was not his suffering that saved the world; it was his loving. And his loving, since it was unconditional, led to great suffering. We too suffer, and our suffering can be very severe. But we must not too quickly identify ourselves with the suffering Jesus. We must always ask ourselves: Am I suffering because I love? Very often suffering can come from being stubborn or angry or wedded to false goals. This kind of suffering has nothing to do with the suffering of Jesus and will not win us salvation with him.

When we read that the soldiers guarding Jesus subjected him to ridicule by dressing him up like a mock king, we are reminded that one of the primary forms of the suffering of Jesus was this attempt to rob him of his dignity. The irony is that he is in fact a king—indeed, the king of kings! But this also means that we, as followers of Jesus, should not be surprised if we too are made fun of or ridiculed for our steadfast trust in God.

I think that this experience is more likely to come our way when we are older and when our faith in God's goodness is thought to be old-fashioned or naïve. Our physical ailments may also cause us to be laughed at, whether it is a loss of memory or some quirky behavior. And then there is always the embarrassment that comes when medical treatment seems to take away all our privacy. We have always taken pride in our ability to take care of ourselves, and now we are often so dependent on others for even the simplest functions, or at least we dread the day when that may happen.

When Pilate presents Jesus, wounded and bound, for all

to see, it is as if the movie is stopped and one frame captures our attention. On one level, this seems to mean: "Look at what happens to misguided idealists!" But on a deeper level, it says: "Look at how much he loves us!" Not only that but, contrary to all human reasoning, this bruised and beaten figure is the most perfect example of human success—not because he is bruised and beaten, but because he has learned how to love without reserve. And we know that such love will guarantee future glory and happiness.

It is very likely that the author of the gospel, writing at the end of the first century, and probably for a Christian community of Asia Minor, sees in the suffering and mocking of Jesus a portrayal of what is happening to his community under Roman persecution. For these Christians, therefore, Pilate's words, "Behold the man," mean, "Behold how we are one with Jesus in being tortured and ridiculed!" Moreover, if that is true, then we too can see ourselves in the person of Jesus when we are rejected or neglected or laughed at because we are patient in our suffering and filled with sure faith in the promises of God.

When we grow old, therefore, we should not be surprised if we feel more and more like Jesus in his suffering and humiliation. But if we persevere and remain positive and hopeful, we can be sure that we will also be one with him in his glorious and eternal resurrection. If we can truly believe that, we will be able to smile at adversity. In fact, by the grace of God, we may even see some humor in our elderly foibles.

54

KNOWING GOD AS LOVING FATHER

If the Spirit of him who raised Jesus from the dead dwells in you, he who raised Christ from the dead will give life to your mortal bodies also through his Spirit that dwells in you…. For all who are led by the Spirit of God are children of God…. When we cry, "Abba! Father!" it is that very Spirit bearing witness with our spirit that we are children of God, and if children, then heirs, heirs of God and joint heirs with Christ—if, in fact, we suffer with him so that we may also be glorified with him (Rom 8:11, 14-17).

It is very difficult for us to imagine how we might have any kind of life that would be different from the life of our present bodies. We may indeed hope that there will be a spiritual life beyond death but that is not what Paul is saying in this passage. He is teaching us, with the guarantee of divine inspiration, that we already possess a spiritual life in this world that is quite separate from the life of our bodies.

This spiritual life is not some half-life that barely survives. It is the life that is given to us by the powerful Spirit of God. If it seems weak, that is only because we have not trusted it and nourished it by faith and prayer. The power of this Spirit is made evident in the fact that it was able to raise Jesus from the dead. We can be sure that this Holy Spirit rejoiced in raising Jesus and that it is more than ready to raise us up also—not only after death, but all through our lives.

The primary effect of this Spirit in us is the unshakable conviction that we have become children of God. Nor must we understand this in some merely metaphorical sense. The Spirit wants us to feel that we belong to God and are loved by God in the same way that children feel that they belong to and can rely on good human parents.

The fruit of this conviction will be a wonderful sense of being claimed and cherished. Children don't have to remind good parents that they belong to the family and can count on love and care. That is simply taken for granted. And it is the same when we belong to the family of God. We all remember how we would come home from school and not have to introduce ourselves or wonder whether there would be something good for us to eat. We might even have had the privilege of checking out the refrigerator. We could simply rejoice in being home and being safe.

We may even have known children who were not as blessed as we were. They lived in a home where there was constant bickering and where they did not feel loved and nourished. They may even have dragged their feet when it came time to leave school. This is a tragic situation but unfortunately it is only too often true.

But this can happen in our relationship with God also. We can well imagine that God is the best and most loving and caring parent that we could ever have. But if we don't know God because we have been too busy to spend time with him, we will not be aware that he is ready to welcome us with open arms. Paul uses the very familiar and intimate name, "Abba," to convey to us the wonderful possibilities of our relationship with this heavenly Father.

When I was returning from my studies in Jerusalem, I was on a ship going to Naples and I overheard a little boy call out to his Jewish father, "Abba! Abba!" Suddenly I understood, in a way that I could never have learned from a book, just how personal and intimate this word could be. There was so much confidence and love in the way that he said it that I was able to understand in some way what Paul meant when he said that we have every right to call out in the same way to our heavenly Father. And then I realized that, no matter how good that boy's father was, he could never match the love and devotion of God for us.

In the ancient world, an inheritance was very important for children. Often this was what gave them a start in life and they could very well end up in real poverty without this help. Paul tells us that our heavenly Father has reserved an inheritance for us that is, as we might imagine, so rich and so bountiful that we can never be able to fully comprehend it. If we are close to Jesus and try to love as he did, it means that we will have to suffer and be patient. But that will soon be over and then we can begin to enjoy the wealth of love and joy that God knows how to give to his faithful children. We should think of this every day…and learn to look ahead with a smile on our faces and in joyful expectation.

55

REJOICING IN THE SPIRIT

Holy Father, protect them in your name that you have given me, so that they may be one, as we are one. While I was with them, I protected them in your name that you have given me.... But now I am coming to you, and I speak these things in the world so that they may have my joy made complete in themselves (John 17:11b-12a, 13).

These words are taken from that final, solemn prayer of Jesus to his heavenly Father on the eve of his passion and death. The words are addressed to his Father but he wants his disciples, and us as well, to hear them and to be consoled by them. When he calls his Father "holy," he is using that term in the biblical sense, not of moral holiness, but of transcendence. God is holy because he is so far above us and so wonderfully unique. He is strong and free and loving in ways that we could never comprehend. But what we can understand is that we need his help. And it is this help that Jesus, his Son, promises to us.

When Jesus asks his Father to protect us "in his name," he is requesting that the powerful name of God be applied to us in a way that will shield us from all possible harm. In the ancient world, the name of a deity was thought to have special power and, in the case of the one supreme God of the Bible, this name was so trustworthy that, when protected by it, one had absolutely no reason to fear anything. And when it is Jesus himself who asks the Father to apply the power of his holy name to us, we can indeed feel surrounded by love and care.

The effect of being protected by the all-powerful name of God is that we can put aside all our competitive impulses. We no longer feel the need to measure ourselves over against others or to wonder whether we are good enough to hold our own. We become like the man in the gospel who found a treasure in his field. Because he felt so rich in this new discovery, he could easily afford to let go of what he had previously thought was indispensable.

We all know how we feel on some days when everything seems to be going wrong, only to experience a kind of liberation from that bondage when we receive some unexpected good news. Suddenly it doesn't matter that someone has said something hurtful about us, or that someone we have competed with has also had good fortune. We are so rich in this new awareness of God's love and goodness, and we feel so protected from all possible bad news, that we can only celebrate our good fortune.

This also reveals the meaning of Jesus' prayer, "so that they may be one, as we are one." This unity, which is like that of the Father and the Son, is not the shallow unity of uniformity. Rather, it is a unity based on the love for one another that characterizes the true Christian community. Such unity is possible because we feel loved by God and are therefore free to love others. This kind of unity also allows us to be our unique selves. In fact, its whole purpose is to make us feel so loved that we are free to be the unique persons that God wants us to be.

I think this is why Jesus says that, even though he is going away and will not be able to protect his disciples as before, he will still be able to guarantee their joy. This is not just because he leaves them a memory of his love and goodness but because he will continue to be with them in a way that is more real and more helpful than was ever possible during the days of his physical presence among them.

This new way in which Jesus is present to the disciples, and to us, is through the Holy Spirit. Jesus may have departed from us in his body but he is powerfully present to us in his Spirit. In John's gospel, this Spirit is called the "Paraclete," which means an "Advocate," that is, one who stands with us in every situation so that we need never feel alone or abandoned. This wonderful Advocate/Spirit is present to our innermost being and is able to convince us that God loves us and will never leave us, unless we push him away.

It is this powerful Spirit who enables us to feel good about ourselves and to put aside thoughts of envy or rivalry. Sometimes we older folks are tempted to feel anger or resentment toward those who are younger or stronger or healthier. The Spirit, if given half a chance, will convince us that we are fine just the way we are. After all, there is no one in the whole world who is quite like each of us. And we need to celebrate that gift of God by loving others and by wishing them well. It is in doing this that we will find true joy in our lives.

56

OUR GOD ABOUNDS IN STEADFAST LOVE

For you, O LORD, are good and forgiving, abounding in steadfast love to all who call on you…. But you, O LORD, are a God merciful and gracious; slow to anger and abounding in steadfast love and faithfulness (Ps 86:5, 15).

One of the most common kinds of human bondage is the burden of guilt. I have a friend who woke up from a nap once and caught himself saying, "Guilty!" Perhaps most of us do not have our subconscious so full of guilt and unworthiness that we are ready to condemn ourselves in such a spontaneous way. But there is little doubt that one of the most deep-seated and persistent causes of sadness and hopelessness is this remembrance of sins or shortcomings for which we do not feel fully forgiven.

I think this is especially the case when we grow older and have more time to think about our past failings and about an imminent judgment. It is then in particular that we are most likely to fall victim to such thoughts of unworthiness and regret. When that happens, we must calmly and patiently reflect on the words of the psalmist who assures us that the Lord is indeed "good and forgiving, abounding in steadfast love" to all who call on him.

When the ancient Israelites reflected on the attributes of the God who had delivered them from bondage, they discovered that his primary attribute was "steadfast love." The God they had come to know was not one who watched to see how they might have failed and was eager to punish them. On the contrary, their God was one who loved them and wanted in every way possible to show them his concern for their freedom and happiness. Only reluctantly did he resort to punishment and then only for the purpose of correcting them and bringing them back to himself.

If there were any doubt on this score, it should be removed forever by those precious words heard by Moses as he came down from Mt. Sinai with the Ten Commandments: "The LORD passed before him, and proclaimed, 'The LORD, the LORD, a God merciful and gracious, slow to anger, and abounding in steadfast love and faithfulness, keeping steadfast love for the thousandth generation, forgiving iniquity and transgression and sin'" (Exod 34:6-7). This is wonderful mathematics indeed! God's loving concern will follow us for a thousand generations, that is, forever. By contrast, as we learn later in the same verse, God will be angry and punish only to the third or fourth generation. What a consolation it is to hear from God himself that his love exceeds his anger by a ratio of one thousand to four! Those are odds that should easily lift a burden from our hearts.

This loving kindness of God is always ready to make allowances and to forgive. We honor God when we remember this. But the Israelites cherished another attribute of God that was second only to his loving, namely, his faithfulness. God is not fickle or inconstant in his loving. On the contrary, when he loves he loves unconditionally and forever. If the covenant with his people is broken, it will not be from God's side. This realization is immensely consoling because we all know how difficult it is for us humans to be faithful in our loving. We often falter and grow tired in our friendships, whereas God is fiercely attentive to all his friends.

As we grow older, we can now see how much better we might have been and how many opportunities for goodness we have missed and, above all, how many hurts to others we could have avoided. But when we recall and repeat these sacred words of the psalmist and thus become more aware of God's love and faithfulness, we ought to be filled with a deep sense of calm and peace. We may rightly regret past actions and attitudes but we must also honor God by taking his words seriously. For it is God himself who has said that he is "merciful and gracious, slow to anger, and abounding in steadfast love and faithfulness."

We do not find it too difficult to believe that God is powerful. After all, he created this universe of ours. But we may very well find it hard to believe in God's goodness…and this may be partly true because he is so powerful. Perhaps the most important message of John's gospel is the assurance from Jesus himself that God cherishes his loving more than his power. As the eternal Word, Jesus came from the bosom of the Father and knows all his secrets. The most important of these is the fact of the Father's love for us. Jesus not only tells us this but he proves it by his own dying for us. In other words, we really need to take seriously the solemn words of Jesus: "For God so loved the world that he gave his only Son, so that everyone who believes in him may not perish but may have eternal life" (John 3:16).

57

JESUS IS OUR RESURRECTION AND OUR LIFE

Now a certain man was ill, Lazarus of Bethany, the village of Mary and her sister Martha…. Jesus loved Martha and her sister and Lazarus…. Jesus said to (Martha), "Your brother will rise again." Martha said to him, "I know that he will rise again in the resurrection on the last day." Jesus said to her, "I am the resurrection and the life. Those who believe in me, even though they die, will live, and everyone who lives and believes in me will never die" (John 11:1, 5, 23-26).

There is something very unusual about the way in which this story about the raising of Lazarus begins. We would expect that the name of the person involved would be given first and then only the specification that he was ill. The fact that John introduces the story in this unusual way indicates that he is really writing about "Everyman" and that the dying Lazarus is simply a representative of all of us who are ill with the incurable disease of mortality. This is, therefore, not just the story of a man who lived many years ago; it is the story of our own problem of making sense out of the inevitable death that awaits us human beings.

This would be a tragic story if it were not for the fact that Jesus loves us just as much as he loved Martha and Mary and Lazarus. In fact, all through this story we are reminded that there is a current of love and concern flowing between Jesus and his three friends. Nothing can be hopeless when the love of Jesus is present.

Martha rushes out to meet Jesus when he approaches their village of Bethany (near Jerusalem). She is distraught at the death of her dear brother and she wonders why Jesus hasn't come in time to prevent this personal tragedy: "Lord, if you had been here, my brother would not have died" (John 11:21). It seems implied also that she wonders why Jesus seems so unconcerned about the death of his own dear friend.

The response of Jesus is meant to be reassuring: "Your brother will rise again" (John 11:23). But Martha sees this as nothing more than a somewhat impersonal reminder of the common belief that there will be a general resurrection at the end of the world. What she is hoping for is an immediate restoration of her dear brother. She is saying, in effect: "I miss him now; I'm not all that interested in eternity."

The response of Jesus is so profound and so uncompromising that we can scarcely comprehend all its implications. He is really making two strong statements about himself and his ability to deal decisively with death. He doesn't just say that he can provide victory over death. He is himself the "resurrection and the life." This can only mean that, if we are united with him, there is no way that death can have the last word in our lives.

This does not mean that Jesus plans to cancel death as a human experience. We are mortal, and dying cannot be avoided. But when we live by the wisdom of Jesus, which means being unselfish in every way we can, death becomes only a transition to a new and better life. In fact, since every act of unselfish love is a little dying to oneself, physical dying also becomes a final act of love as we trust God and look to him beyond the darkness. If our lives are filled with loving and caring—and therefore the many ways of dying to self—we will have no real difficulty with the final moment of dying. It is only the selfish and self-centered person who will find it very difficult to let go at the end.

The way that we can participate in this life-giving power of Jesus is through our faith. As Jesus told Martha, "Those who believe in me, even though they die, will live." But we must constantly remind ourselves that believing in Jesus does not mean simply that we agree that he lived many years ago in Palestine, or that he worked miracles, or even that he died and rose again. All these facts are very important and are part of our believing. However, to believe in a way that leads to our own resurrection means nothing less than to embrace unreservedly the teaching of Jesus about the necessity of living unselfishly.

In other words, we must have the kind of faith that really changes our lives from our natural tendency to think primarily of ourselves to a new kind of life where we are sensitive to the situation of others and where we are kind and thoughtful and forgiving. It is far from easy to undergo this kind of conversion and it requires our constant attention. As we grow older and are afflicted with all kinds of weaknesses, we will naturally tend to be preoccupied with our own concerns. But that is when we should try hardest to live out the command of Jesus to love one another. There are few things more beautiful than the picture of an older person who is constantly attentive to the welfare of others. Such a one will never need to fear death.

58

RESURRECTION ALLOWS US TO LAUGH AT DEATH

For if the dead are not raised, then Christ has not been raised. If Christ has not been raised, your faith is futile and you are still in your sins.... If the dead are not raised, "Let us eat and drink, for tomorrow we die" .... When this perishable body puts on imperishability, and this mortal body puts on immortality, then the saying that is written will be fulfilled: "Death has been swallowed up in victory." "Where, O death, is your victory? Where, O death, is your sting" (1 Cor 15:16-17, 32, 54-55)?

When Paul says that the dead will be raised, he means not only that we will continue to live after death but, even more surprisingly, that our bodies will be restored to us in some miraculous and wonderful way. We cannot possibly understand how this can happen but we do have the authority of the inspired scriptures to support this conclusion. These will be our very own bodies, but without all the frailties of the bodies we now have. I am sure, for example, that my father, who was almost totally deaf for the last twenty years of his life, will hear perfectly in his risen body.

Paul knows how difficult it will be for us to believe this in view of the condition of some bodies after death. That is why he does not hesitate to equate the certainty of our bodily resurrection with the absolute certainty of the resurrection of Jesus. In fact, the whole basis of our faith will collapse if our bodily resurrection turns out to be a false promise.

In that case we are reduced to the desperate condition of the non-believers who, concluding that there is no life beyond this one, have no choice but to make the most of the brief life they do possess. Their philosophy of despair is aptly expressed in the pagan advice, "Let us eat and drink, for tomorrow we die." Such a philosophy makes some sense to the young and the strong, and unfortunately many of them adopt it, but for those who are old and growing weak it can only mean the victory of darkness.

Fortunately, every word in the Bible rejects this philosophy of despair and affirms with certainty the hope that God has instilled in us and that is meant to grow ever stronger as we approach the end of this life. For it is then that, as Paul assures us, "this perishable body will put on imperishability, and this mortal body will put on immortality." The fact that we cannot readily imagine how this can happen does not in any way diminish the certainty of it.

Christ himself is the guarantor of this promise. For we recall the wonderfully comforting words of Paul in 2 Corinthians: "For the Son of God, Jesus Christ, whom we proclaimed among you…was not 'Yes and No'; but in him it is always 'Yes.' For in him every one of God's promises is a 'Yes'" (1:19-20). This is the make-or-break issue for believers. We may believe a thousand things about the Bible and perform a thousand rituals in our churches, but if we do not believe that Jesus rose from the dead and that we also will rise at the end of time, all is lost.

We do not see Paul wavering on this issue. In fact, he is so certain about the resurrection of both Jesus and ourselves that he dares to taunt that formidable foe we call death. Death has the power to cast a shadow back over our lives so that we can never seem to be liberated from its threatening presence. At times the fear of death is so strong that we are rendered almost immobile. We no longer want to initiate any new projects or make any new friends, so great is the threat of death, especially in our later years.

But Paul assures us that "death has been swallowed up in victory." In the resurrection of Jesus, when for the first time a tomb was opened from the inside, the power of death was exposed as mostly bluster. It is like the Wizard of Oz who scared the wits out of little Dorothy and her companions until they discovered that he was nothing but an old man punching buttons on a console! Jesus has also unmasked the real nature of death. It is no longer the end of everything but the beginning of our new and much better life.

We too then should join Paul in making fun of this old enemy that has been rendered helpless by the loving and dying of Jesus: "Where, O death, is your victory? Where, O death, is your sting?" The only thing that should claim our attention is our own devotion to that loving service which will deliver us from the power of evil. And the more we are delivered from the fear of death, the more we will be free to be a loving presence no matter where we may be or how difficult life may seem to be.

59

Thirsting for the Lord

O God, you are my God, I seek you, my soul thirsts for you; my flesh faints for you, as in a dry and weary land where there is no water (Ps 63:1).

The psalmist uses striking images to express the condition of persons who have come to know and love the Lord but who, like many lovers, are deeply affected by the apparent absence of the one they love. Love seeks perfect union but that is impossible in our present condition. And so loving is a bittersweet experience with moments of deep communion separated by periods of yearning and fruitless seeking.

Someone has observed that the most common characteristic of us human beings is that we are forever searching for someone or something. This is expressed in our literature in such stories as the search for the Holy Grail or for the hidden paradise of Shangri-La.

This awareness is found everywhere in Scripture. We see it, for example, in the story of the two disciples of the Baptist who decided to follow Jesus. Jesus turned to them and asked, "What are you looking for" (John 1:38)? I think he could just as easily have said, "You must be humans, for I see that you are forever searching for something!" When they respond, "Where are you staying?" Jesus says to them, "Come and see" (John 1:39).

The clear implication of this exchange is that Jesus is not really "staying" anywhere. He is on a journey, and he invites the disciples (and all of us) to follow him. Since we can do so only by loving as he does, we inevitably fall behind. Nonetheless, we very much want to be with him and so, as we try to keep up, we feel an aching void and that can cause us to think that we have been abandoned. We have all seen this happen when a small child tries to walk with adults and is always in danger of being left behind!

This sense of being separated from the one we love is conveyed by the graphic images of the psalmist. He must have been a deeply spiritual person or he would not have known about this experience of "presence in absence," which is both wonderful and painful. He says that his soul "thirsts" for God. Anyone who has been really thirsty knows how persistent this feeling of dryness can be. As the psalmist says, it is indeed like a "dry and weary land where there is no water." He imagines his throat and tongue to be like land that is dusty and cracked because of a severe drought.

I like to do a little gardening in my spare time. It helps me to stay in touch with my youth as a farm boy in the mountains of western Pennsylvania. And so I know from experience how frustrating it is to see all one's labor compromised by a severe drought. The plants, and the soil itself, seem to be crying out for moisture. Even the weeds are having a hard time. The ground actually cracks open as if pleading for at least a brief shower.

The psalmist knew about this too, for he lived in a country where rainfall is very scarce. When I was a student in Jerusalem,

I recall how amazed I was to discover that it never rained there from May until October. And when the winter rains fail to arrive, the crops wither. In ancient Israel, that would mean famine and death. No wonder, then, that the psalmist uses personal experience as a guide in trying to describe the yearning of his soul for his divine friend who seems to be so far away.

Sometimes we are so busy, especially in our younger years, that we have no time to listen to the quiet voice of God. We can become so absorbed in the problems of this world that we don't have time, or don't take time, to think about that other world where we really belong. But as we grow older, we come to realize that there is much more to life than what this world offers. If we are lucky, we will acknowledge that painful void and turn to the One who alone is able to fill it. Hopefully, we will then recognize that the experience of this aloneness is actually a healthy reminder that we should pay more attention to what is really important in our lives.

Paul tells us that "God has sent the Spirit of his Son into our hearts, crying, 'Abba! Father!'" (Gal 4:6). This divine Spirit actually causes us to become homesick, as it were, for our true home where alone we will find peace and security. And so we must learn to pray with the Spirit that we may be led to that homeland for which we are supposed to be yearning. If we are patient and persistent in our prayers, God will reveal to us the reality of a loving Father waiting with open arms to welcome us into his blessed kingdom.

60

JESUS SHOWS US HOW TO PRAY

But now more than ever the word about Jesus spread abroad; many crowds would gather to hear him and to be cured of their diseases. But he would withdraw to deserted places and pray (Luke 5:15-16). *Now during those days he went out to the mountain to pray; and he spent the night in prayer to God* (Luke 6:12).

In the early days of Jesus' ministry, he spoke to the crowds about the coming of God's kingdom and he established his credibility by working miracles. There are few things that are more appealing than giving people good news and backing it up with signs of God's approval. As a consequence, large crowds began to gather and to press in upon Jesus so that even his disciples asked him at times to send the people away. It is not easy to be a celebrity.

But the way that Jesus dealt with this problem was, not to send people away, but to go away himself to some deserted place where he could speak to his heavenly Father about what was happening to him and to the crowds that followed him. This heavenly Father had spoken those powerful, liberating words to him at his baptism, "You are my Son, the Beloved" (Mark 1:11), and so he looked for opportunities to be present to that loving Father and to hear again that he was chosen and special.

In those early days, he must have told his Father about his wonderful successes and about the enthusiasm of the people who heard him. But then he would have noticed that not all in the crowds were cheering. On the fringes of the gatherings there would have been Scribes and Pharisees and emissaries from the Jerusalem temple who would have been spying on him and would not have been pleased with the apparently Messianic pretensions of one who had not checked with them first. They would have told him that he could not work miracles on the Sabbath and they would be shaking their heads, therefore, in disapproval. Jesus could not simply ignore them, for they represented power in a way that the crowd of simple folk did not.

Jesus would surely have spoken to his Father about all this and would have been reassured. And then a cold chill must have gripped Jesus as he received word that his cousin, John the Baptist, had been put to death. He must have noted with alarm that God had apparently not changed the way that he deals with his prophets. For most of them had died for the sake of their message. But he too was God's prophet with the ultimate message of God about the salvation of his beloved people.

Some may wonder how Jesus could feel this way since he is divine as well as human and therefore should know everything. But we must remember that he is truly human and that he put aside his divine privileges for the sake of his humanity and for the sake of our own communion with him. Paul makes this clear when he writes to the Philippians that Jesus, "though he was in the form of God, did not regard equality with God as something to be exploited, but emptied himself, taking the form of a slave, being born in human likeness" (2:6-7). If this is so, it means that Jesus (like ourselves) truly did grow in his awareness of what his mission would require of him.

We can assume, therefore, that Jesus not only talked about the good news of his popularity in those long moments with his Father, but that he also brought the more threatening news about the hostility of the Jerusalem hierarchy and the fate of John the Baptist. And we can also be sure that his loving Father told him once again that "You are my Son, the Beloved."

It was about this time that Jesus told his disciples that "the Son of Man must undergo great suffering" (Mark 8:31). He was now convinced that he was not to save the world by leading a rebellion and by killing Roman soldiers. Rather, he would do so in the way of divine wisdom: by loving, and therefore suffering, and therefore dying, and therefore rising to new life in the glory of his Father's presence.

We humans tend to think that all problems can be solved by power, whether it is our own superior strength or military force or the psychic violence that can make other people feel inferior. But Jesus tells us, in word and in deed, that the only power that has lasting and blessed effects is the unlikely but invincible power of unselfish love.

It is surely about this mission of love that Jesus spoke to his Father in those long silent nights in Galilee. It is also this kind of love that we should ask for in the long, quiet days and nights of our later years. For this love will make us stronger than all the efforts of our days of youth and human strength. And this kind of love will lead us, with Jesus, to resurrection glory.

61

DISCOVERING MARY AS SPIRITUAL MOTHER

When Jesus saw his mother and the disciple whom he loved standing beside her, he said to his mother, "Woman, here is your son." Then he said to the disciple, "Here is your mother." And from that hour the disciple took her into his own home (John 19:26-27).

This passage is especially noteworthy because it brings together two important and unnamed persons in John's gospel. The mother of Jesus is never called "Mary" in this gospel and "the disciple whom he loved" is never given a personal name either. This cannot be an accident or an oversight. The only plausible conclusion is that the author wants us to see these two persons, not just as historical or dated figures, but also as having a powerful and perennial symbolic meaning.

In this regard, we must be careful to note that "symbolic" does not mean unreal or imaginary; it means significant in a way that goes far beyond the immediate historical fact of the existence of these two persons. The opposite of symbolic is not unreal but meaningless. Therefore, one does not have to question the historical possibility of this exchange at the foot of the cross in order to look for the deeper symbolic meaning of these two persons for our own understanding of what is at issue in the dying of Jesus.

It is no accident that John's gospel begins with the phrase, "In the beginning." This alerts us to the fact that the author sees his gospel as a kind of new Genesis, as God sends his divine Word (his "Fiat") to bring about a new creation. This also sheds light on the fact that Jesus calls his mother, "Woman," not only here but also at the feast of Cana (John 2:4). This tells us that the evangelist sees in Mary a new Eve, who in Genesis is called the "mother of all living" (3:20).

In the spiritual realm, this makes Mary the symbolic embodiment of the Church, which through baptism brings forth new members for the Christian community. By the same token, the "disciple whom Jesus loved" is the symbolic embodiment of all who are reborn in baptism and are entrusted to the loving care of Mary/Church. Mary was the physical mother of Jesus and now she receives from her Son the mandate and privilege of being the spiritual mother of all who are made one with him in baptism.

Conversely, all those who have committed themselves to Christ in baptism become brothers and sisters of the "disciple whom Jesus loved." By implication, they become also the "beloved ones," a title that should be the source of wonderful comfort and encouragement for all of us. We could scarcely imagine a more privileged vocation than to be called to join the beloved disciple and the mother of Jesus at this final, climactic moment in the drama of salvation.

There is something else about this scene that is worth pondering. In John's gospel, Jesus is very self-possessed even in the darkest moments of his passion. It seems clear that, as he senses his imminent departure, he wishes to make provision for the people whom he loves and from whom he is now departing. In Matthew's gospel, Jesus makes provision for authority and order in the Church as he names apostles and assigns to Peter a special role as "keeper of the keys." John's gospel is far more concerned with the more mystical and charismatic dimension of the Church.

This means that emphasis will be placed on the loving relationships implied in the roles of "mother" and "son/child." It is important that there be a legitimately established order in the Christian community lest the welfare of the Church be compromised by division and chaos. At the same time, there must be room to breathe, as it were, so that the prophetic and poetic side of the Church is given its due. For it is in the company of prophets and poets that we find the inspiration without which we are apt to succumb to tedium and boredom.

We older folks need to be especially sensitive to this balance. Most of us are probably more concerned with order than we are with creativity. For that reason, we need to nourish consciously the poetic side of our natures. Then perhaps people will apply to us the words of Peter in the Acts of the Apostles (quoting the prophet Joel): "In the last days it will be, God declares, that I will pour out my Spirit upon all flesh, and your sons and your daughters shall prophesy, and your young men shall see visions, and your old men (and women) shall dream dreams" (2:17). Thus all the people will be inspired and delighted.

62

THE HIDDEN TREASURE OF GOD'S PRESENCE

But we have this treasure in clay jars, so that it may be made clear that this extraordinary power belongs to God and does not come from us. We are afflicted in every way, but not crushed; perplexed, but not driven to despair; persecuted, but not forsaken; struck down, but not destroyed; always carrying in the body the death of Jesus, so that the life of Jesus may also be made visible in our bodies (2 Cor 4:7-10).

In Paul's day, clay or earthen jars were the normal way to transport expensive liquids, such as wine or olive oil. Ancient shipwrecks often reveal a cargo of such jars. Paul finds this image helpful in explaining the situation of believers, who possess, in fragile human bodies, the most precious of all contents—a knowledge and love of God, revealed by the presence of Jesus.

We know this from an earlier verse where Paul says, "For it is the God who said, 'Let light shine out of darkness,' who has shone in our hearts to give the light of the knowledge of the glory of God in the face of Jesus Christ" (2 Cor 4:6). This precious gift of faith is thus likened to the light of the original creation, which has the power to dispel all darkness and which now glows warmly in our hearts. This same light shone in the face of Jesus at the Transfiguration and prepared him for his final act of love and sacrifice.

This treasure is a gift of God, for only God can provide the ability to face the darkness with unconquerable hope and trust. And we carry this precious cargo in the clay jars of our mortal bodies. If we have reached a certain age, there is no need to explain what this means! For clay jars are easily broken and must therefore be handled with great care, just as we know how easy it is for our own "clay jars" to begin to ache and stiffen.

Nonetheless, these bodies are more than capable of serving the purpose intended by our Creator. They were never meant to be more than temporary containers, which sooner or later must be broken in order to release their precious contents into the mighty river of God's love and goodness. In the meantime, our bodies enable us to show the love and kindness that are the inevitable fruit of that divine light that illumines the deepest recesses of our being.

Examples of this inner glow-made-visible are the smiles that appear on our faces and the tender touches of our fingers as we reach out to others in loving service. The fact that the smile is on a wrinkled face or the touch is from an arthritic hand merely enhances the love and concern that they manifest. These are, in some ways, little copies of the "glory of God in the face of Jesus" about which Paul writes.

Paul then attempts to describe some of the experiences of human frailty, which beset him. He is "afflicted...perplexed... persecuted...struck down." We can easily make our own list of afflictions. We may be in pain or depressed or hopeless or feel abandoned. Unfortunately, we usually remind ourselves, and tell others, about our problems so often that we have no difficulty in listing them.

But we must be careful to note that Paul sees all his problems in the context of God's presence and assistance: he is also "not crushed…not driven to despair…not forsaken…not destroyed." Paul is no Pollyanna, who denies the presence of evil and pain and despair in the world. Denial of pain and misery and death is no solution. But with that realism we must recognize the equally sure reality of the presence and goodness of our loving, gentle and merciful God.

Paul recognizes this when he says that we are "carrying in the body the death of Jesus." This means that we are experiencing not only the physical weakness of all human bodies but that we are, if truly followers of Jesus, experiencing also the sacrifices that come from caring about others. And when we are in fact such loving, caring persons, we are making it possible that "the life of Jesus may also be made visible in our bodies."

There are few sights more beautiful in this world of ours than that of older persons who, in spite of frailty and suffering and dependence on others, are able to bear witness to the kindness and thoughtfulness and patience that show forth that inner presence of God. This is indeed the "life of Jesus…made visible in our bodies." It is true that we may not be able to bear such witness every day but, if we see it as an ideal, there is a good chance that we will be able, most of the time, to make Christ present in such a beautiful and helpful way.

63

ALLOWING GOD'S WAYS
TO BE MYSTERIOUS

David said to his servants, "Is the child dead?" They said, "He is dead." Then David rose from the ground, washed, anointed himself, and changed his clothes…. Then his servants said to him, "What is this thing that you have done? You fasted and wept for the child while it was alive; but when the child died, you rose and ate food." He said, "While the child was still alive, I fasted and wept; for I said, 'Who knows? The LORD may be gracious to me, and the child may live.' But now he is dead; why should I fast? Can I bring him back again? I shall go to him, but he will not return to me" (2 Sam 12:19b-23).

There is something very poignant about this scene of the powerful King David accepting the news of the death of his infant son. This was the child of his illicit union with Bathsheba, which led also to the murder of Uriah. David knew that the prophet Nathan was right in telling him that he would be punished by having that precious child taken from him. But he hoped and prayed that God would relent and demand something less dear to him than this child which was the son of the first woman he had ever really loved.

Nonetheless, the child did die. The officials of his court were afraid to tell him. They said, "While the child was still alive, we spoke to him, and he did not listen to us; how then can we tell him the child is dead? He may do himself some harm" (2 Sam 12:18). So they gathered at the door of the king's apartment, each urging the other to be the bearer of bad news. They may very well have feared that the king would lash out at the one who told him what he did not want to hear. But it did not take David long to guess what was happening: "But when David saw that his servants were whispering together, he perceived that the child was dead" (2 Sam 12:19).

Up to this moment, everything was happening according to normal expectations. But now there is a sudden change. The king did not begin to wail and to throw the furniture about the room and to cry out, "Why did this have to happen to me? I don't know whether I can still believe in God. For God has shown me that he is not really my friend. I don't think I can go to church any longer!" The fact that the death of the child is connected with David's sinfulness does not change matters that much. He might have said, "Punish me for my sin. But taking my child is in no way proportionate to my guilt."

As we grow older, we can all remember occasions when we thought God was acting toward us in a way that was hardly compatible with his great love and mercy. We may even have become alienated from God—in our hearts, and perhaps even in our external behavior. In many cases, this happens when a child has died or been permanently disabled. Or perhaps some beloved parent or dear friend has been taken away while still in the prime of life. The longer we live, the more likely it is that we will have to deal with the painful mystery of God's ways in our lives.

At this stage, it is important to note that King David is not just an historical personage from the Old Testament. He is also a symbolic figure, which means that he represents in many of his actions and attitudes a model for all believers. The biblical author signals this by emphasizing certain elements in the story of King David. This happens with other figures also. For example, just as King David represents an attitude of faith in the presence of tragedy, so does King Saul represent the lack of faith in the tragedy of his own life, which ended in suicide.

And so we are asked to relate, not only to the suffering of David at the death of his infant son, but also to the reaction of David as he accepted the will of God and decided to get on with his life. He was able to do so, not because he understood, but because he had come to trust God, in bad times as well as in good. He knew that the death of his child was God's will and that he must try to accept that because God has been good to him on many other occasions.

When we ponder their implications, the final words of David are truly amazing for a man who lived almost a thousand years before Christ. The revelation that there would be reward and punishment after this life did not come until hundreds of years after David. Yet, drawing on his strong faith and his sense of God's goodness, he is able to say, "I shall go to (the child), but he will not return to me." In other words, the good God whom I trust will keep my child safe, but only on condition that I return to the duties and obligations of my life, as God expects me to do. In other words, grieving is unavoidable, but life must go on…and we must make the most of it.

64

POOR NOW AND RICH FOREVER

Blessed are you who are poor, for yours is the kingdom of God. Blessed are you who are hungry now, for you will be filled. Blessed are you who weep now, for you will laugh (Luke 6:20b-21).

When Jesus declares that the "poor" are blessed or fortunate, he is not extolling poverty as such. This becomes clear when we consider the special meaning of the word, "poor," in the Bible. It referred originally to those Israelites who, in the last centuries of the Old Testament, clung to their belief in God's power and goodness even as they were being oppressed by foreign powers and seemingly abandoned by the once powerful God of the Exodus. In the Old Testament, the literal translation of this word is "the afflicted ones," for this is how they felt under foreign oppression.

When we consider the circumstances of these "afflicted ones," we notice that their most obvious problem was that they were powerless. They felt completely helpless in regard to such fundamental factors of life as security, hope and political autonomy. They wanted to believe in the power and goodness of God but in their misery they could see no evidence of God's concern for them. Even the prophets had disappeared. How they wished to hear even the scolding prophets—anything but this deadly silence!

When we grow older, we begin to realize how powerless we really are. Medical science is helpful but we know that even its special promise will eventually disappoint us. We wonder why God has given us such a yearning for life only to let it slip away from us. As our strength begins to ebb, we can easily identify with the powerless ones of this Beatitude.

In this situation, Jesus tells us without qualification that when we grow weak we should consider ourselves blessed or fortunate…in spite of everything. How can this be? From God's perspective, it makes a lot of sense. We think that losing our strength is a terrible thing. But God wants to wean us away from a reliance on our strength, which was never meant to last, so that we will begin to trust in his strength, which will last forever. After all, it is an illusion to think that our own strength will ever bring us real and lasting success and happiness. Accordingly, those who begin to lose their strength are actually being delivered from a deadly illusion that can only lead to terrible disappointment.

But Jesus is not just reminding us of the reality of our fragile condition. He tells us also that, if we accept our weakness and begin to put our faith in the power of God, he will respond by giving us the Kingdom! And this Kingdom is a gift whose dimensions we will never be able to comprehend. I have my own translation of this word that occurs so often in the gospels: Even more than being the final victory of God's power it is God's dream for his beloved children! This is so much better for us than anything that our own power or dreaming could ever achieve. And when it happens, we will never want to go back to our previous reliance on a power that is no power.

In the light of this understanding of the first Beatitude, we can also see why Jesus would continue and declare, "Blessed are you who are hungry now, for you will be filled." In the ancient world, hunger was a constant companion and so they could readily understand that physical hunger is only a preview of the deeper hunger for peace and happiness. This hunger grows ever more acute as we lose our strength (and sometimes our appetite). But if we trust the promise of Jesus, we will be "filled," that is, we will acquire a deep spiritual satisfaction that results from putting all our trust in a good and merciful God.

Finally, Jesus assures us that we are blessed if we "weep now," for this is only a preparation for the time when we will laugh. Those who weep now are the blessed ones who have dared to love generously and who thus allow themselves to become vulnerable. In fact, as we have probably noticed, those who love will soon learn how to grieve. Nonetheless, for all its heartache, such a situation is so much better than not loving at all. And what Jesus promises is that, when we love and invest our lives in the welfare of others, we will eventually laugh heartily as tears of joy stream down our wrinkled faces! And what a wonderful mirth that will be.

It is so important that we meditate frequently on these Beatitudes because this is the only way that we will be able to counteract the pervasive and destructive philosophy of our secular world where the only thing that counts is power and control. In the days of our weakness and loss of control, it is so comforting to learn that our loving Lord is ready and willing to supply all the strength that we will ever need…and for eternity.

65

HEARING JESUS CALL US BY NAME

(Mary Magdalene) turned around and saw Jesus standing there, but she did not know that it was Jesus. Jesus said to her, "Woman, why are you weeping? Whom are you looking for?" Supposing him to be the gardener, she said to him, "Sir, if you have carried him away, tell me where you have laid him, and I will take him away." Jesus said to her, "Mary!" She turned and said to him in Hebrew, "Rabbouni!" (which means Teacher) (John 20:14b-16).

We all recognize this as one of the appearances of Jesus after his resurrection. But this is the only time that he appears to a single person and the dialogue is profoundly personal. We already know from the earlier verses that Mary Magdalene had gone to the tomb of Jesus and, finding it empty, had seen two angels there. They asked her why she was weeping. But they did not tell her that the tomb was empty because Jesus was risen from the dead, as they did in the other gospel accounts (see Mark 16:5-6).

This may seem like a rather small difference. However, throughout John's gospel there is a constant insistence on the need for a personal, mystical union with God, in Jesus and through the power of the Holy Spirit. Therefore, it will not do at all to have Mary hear about the most important event in the life of her friend simply by the witness of third parties, even if they are angels! This great good news must come from the lips of Jesus himself. (We too know that when we have really good news we want to announce it to our dearest friends in person).

Jesus seems to have been disguised in some way, because Mary thinks that he is the gardener. Or it may simply be that she didn't expect to see him there. In any case, she does not recognize him until he addresses her by name. We would love to have been there and to have heard the special accent on that word, "Mary," but we can be sure that it was spoken in a most personal and tender way. And we can scarcely imagine the surprise and joy that filled the heart of Mary herself. She can only exclaim, "Rabbouni," which was undoubtedly the address that she used throughout her association with Jesus, for he was the beloved Master and she was his ardent student.

This touching little story has some most important implications for our own relationship with God. In fact, I think it is fair to say that we will have missed the most significant event of our lives, if we have not heard Jesus address us also by our personal names, and if we have not been able to respond with the same fervor and joy that we hear in the response of Mary Magdalene.

If we have had the good fortune to be brought up in a religious household, we will have been taught about the proper way to relate to God. We will have learned prayers, such as the Our Father and the Hail Mary, and we will have become accustomed to attending church and observing many other rituals which had the purpose of making us aware of God's presence in our lives. If this is true, we have truly been blessed and are well on our way to the experience of a deeply spiritual and satisfying life.

At some point, however, we should have begun to understand that there is much more to religion than religious words and acts. These are in fact merely a good beginning. They are meant to lead us to a deeply personal relationship with the God whom we have been honoring by our prayers and ritual acts. To put it plainly, religious words and acts must never be an end in themselves but are intended to lead us to a mystical experience of God's presence in all the aspects of our lives.

That is why it would never have been sufficient for Mary Magdalene to hear about the resurrection of Jesus from two angels, any more than it would be sufficient for us to know Jesus only as one about whom our parents or teachers have spoken to us. We surely need that witness too, but it is meant only to lead us to the time when we hear the voice of Jesus speaking our personal names with exquisite tenderness and love.

I think this challenge is especially strong for those of us who are getting along in years. We need to continue to pray in our customary ways, but we should also give ourselves a chance to be with Jesus in a way that is beyond words. We need to be simply in his presence and to hear him calling us by name and reassuring us that we are loved and will never be forgotten. This will surely bring us a wonderful experience of peace and trust at a time when we need it more than ever before in our lives.

66

GOD CAN MAKE US STRONGER IN OUR WEAKNESS

Three times I appealed to the Lord about this, that it would leave me, but he said to me, "My grace is sufficient for you, for power is made perfect in weakness." So I will boast all the more gladly of my weaknesses, so that the power of Christ may dwell in me. Therefore I am content with weaknesses, insults, hardships, persecutions, and calamities for the sake of Christ; for whenever I am weak, then I am strong (2 Cor 12:8-10).

A great quantity of scholarly ink has been spilled trying to identify this problem that plagued Paul. Some think it may have been a stubborn physical ailment; others prefer to see in it some psychological problem. While we would like to know more about it, we must agree with Paul that the exact nature of the ailment is not important. What is important is our recognition that Paul, brilliant and resourceful as he was, still shared in a significant way in the frailty of our common human condition.

We know how many times we have prayed for help in some threatening situation and we know that our prayers have often been answered. However, we are also aware that, sooner or later, the threat we face will turn out to be as bad as, or perhaps even worse than, we had feared. At that time, we should read what Paul has to say here about the real meaning of strength and weakness.

God's response to Paul's plea for help is comforting but paradoxical. First he promises Paul that his help will be available. Then, however, he makes the surprising claim that "power is made perfect in weakness." The implication is that Paul's weakness provides a better opportunity for God's power to work in him than his recovery ever could.

The point is that, when our own strength fails, we must turn to God for help, and God will then use this opening to make us strong with his strength rather than with our own. The end result is that we are indeed much stronger in that case than we ever could have been without this reliance on God's help.

Rather than boasting about his own strength, Paul realizes that he has more reason to boast about the much greater strength that God has loaned him. Now his weakness is not a problem, because it has made it possible for the "power of Christ" to dwell in him. We will never be able to understand what Paul means here until we experience it in our own lives. But we must first of all believe that this can happen to us and not just to Paul.

Therefore, when our prayers for recovery are not answered, it does not mean that God has ignored our plea. Rather, this situation provides a golden opportunity to accept our weakness, whatever it may be, and to ask God to provide a new and better kind of strength. This new strength from God may be the ability to accept cheerfully what is happening, or it may help us to feel more compassionate toward others who are also suffering. It is amazing how often an illness can challenge our smugness and self-sufficiency. In this way, we can become more sensitive and caring persons than would ever have happened without this trial.

Paul is not making things up when he lists some of the hardships that he has faced in his career as a missionary. We can make our own list, but the hardships provided by Paul can be very similar to the ones that we might claim. We can easily relate to what Paul calls "weaknesses." There are times when we can hardly hold up our heads and when our feet won't take us where we want to go.

We know what is meant by "insults" also. People can be cruel at times and even unintentional comments can be very hurtful. Others may find it difficult to be patient with our slowness or with our poor hearing or eyesight. We may feel that we are not likely to suffer "persecution," but I have always felt that the Bible has a broader definition of persecution than we are accustomed to. I think it includes attempts to ridicule or make fun of our faith, claiming that we are naïve or gullible or even misguided. This is surely the case in that final Beatitude where Jesus tells us that those are blessed who suffer persecution (Matthew 5:11), which certainly includes being ridiculed for their faith and their moral idealism.

Finally, Paul sums it all up with his famous statement that "whenever I am weak, then I am strong." In the light of what we have already said, it is clear that Paul is not extolling weakness as such. But he does tell us that when our weakness makes room for God's strength we are stronger than we ever could be, even on our best days.

67

OPENING OUR HEARTS
TO GOD'S LOVE

O come, let us sing to the LORD.... *Let us come into his
presence with thanksgiving.... O come, let us worship and bow
down, let us kneel before the* LORD, *our Maker! For he is our
God, and we are the people of his pasture, and the sheep of
his hand. O that today you would listen to his voice! Do not
harden your hearts, as at Meribah, as on the day at Massah in
the wilderness, when your ancestors tested me, and put me to
the proof, though they had seen my work* (Ps 95:1-2, 6-9).

St. Benedict was one of the most influential masters of the
spiritual life in all of Christendom. He wrote his Rule for monks
in the early sixth century and he was profoundly influenced
by earlier monastic traditions. The Benedictine monasteries
that flourished in the early Middle Ages were influential in pre-
serving the wisdom of the Bible to which they were entirely
devoted. St. Benedict prescribed that this Psalm 95 should be
recited every day by his monks as an introduction to the prayers
that were said in the very early morning. This was their invari-
able greeting of the new day.

This example of the early monks is a model for all Christians. The first thought as we rise from sleep should be of that attentive God who has been watching over us during the hours of sleep. No matter how strong or how weak we may feel at that early hour, we need to say, "Let us sing to the Lord…. Let us worship and bow down, let us kneel before the Lord, our Maker!" For we really are creatures who depend for every breath on this Creator, whose love caused him to make the world, and who was able to survey all that he had made and declare it "very good" (Genesis 1:31).

It is so important that we begin each day with a positive appreciation of the goodness in life, in spite of much evil and frequent illness. In a very real sense, we are able to choose what kind of a day it will be. If we bless it and thank God for it, we will be able to see the goodness that it can bring us. By the same token, if we begin the day with an admission of defeat in the presence of evil, we will never be able to allow God's love to lift us above the problems in our lives and enable us to see the goodness that is often hidden from those who are not able to trust the Lord.

Part of this "greeting" of the Lord must also be an expression of gratitude for the many blessings of the past: "Let us come into his presence with thanksgiving; let us make a joyful noise to him with songs of praise!" (Ps 95:2). On some days, this "joyful noise" will seem like singing in the rain, but we know that such singing is the only way to assure that we will see the sun after the rain has passed. Those of us who are getting on in years should be especially aware of the many blessings for which we should be grateful; we really need to acquire the habit of counting our blessings.

When we do remember the good things in our past, we will also be able to say with the psalmist: "For he is our God, and we are the people of his pasture, and the sheep of his hand." We should try very hard to appreciate the imagery here even if it is drawn from the unfamiliar life of the shepherd. The sheep depend entirely on the dedication of their shepherd. He can lead them to water and to pasture. When danger threatens, he is there to protect them. They know that they will not survive without his devotion to their welfare. The psalmist wants us to feel that way about God. And he assures us that God feels that way about us.

Unfortunately, we are all too inclined to disregard the presence of our Shepherd. We think we can do quite well all by ourselves, or only with those who agree with us. But this is a recipe for disaster—for the sheep, and also for us. Therefore, the psalmist pleads with us to avoid the mistakes of ancient Israel: "O that today you would listen to his voice! Do not harden your hearts, as at Meribah, as on the day of Massah in the wilderness." These two names are code words for Israel's resistance to Moses and to God (see Exodus 17:1-7).

As we grow older, we may find it more difficult to heed the guidance of our divine Shepherd. His wise direction may seem useless or even foolish. Why should we try to be nice to others when we don't feel well and have so little hope? But we must not harden our hearts. Now more than ever we need the loving care and attention of that ever faithful and loving Shepherd. Our secular culture places a premium on an attitude of self-sufficiency. But that is not reality. In fact it is both foolish and tragic if we realize too late that our Lord has always been ready to some to our assistance. Let us not harden our hearts to God's gracious concern for us.

68

THE DIFFICULTY—AND THE BEAUTY—OF FORGIVENESS

Love your enemies, do good to those who hate you, bless those who curse you, pray for those who abuse you…. If you love those who love you, what credit is that to you? For even sinners love those who love them…. Be merciful, just as your Father is merciful. Do not judge, and you will not be judged; do not condemn, and you will not be condemned. Forgive, and you will be forgiven; give and it will be given to you. A good measure, pressed down, shaken together, running over, will be put into your lap (Luke 6:27-28, 32, 36-38).

When we hear these words of Jesus, we are surely inclined to say, Dear Lord, you can't possibly be serious! How can you expect poor, weak mortals like us to live according to such lofty ideals? But the words of Jesus are unmistakable and their challenge is only too real.

Jesus knows that we are weak; in fact, he knows it better than we do; but he also knows that his love can strengthen us so that we will be able to do things that are far beyond our normal capacity. Jesus not only gives us the command to love our enemies but he also gives us the ability to do so. In fact, his very own loving can join our feeble efforts and thus enable us to love our enemies just as he loves everyone, good or bad.

It is only too true that we often limit our loving to our friends; but then we hear Jesus saying that such carefully focused and restrictive loving is putting us on the same level as the pagans. Surely that is not a comfortable place to be. The conclusion is inescapable: To be followers of Jesus, we must love as he did, and that is an unconditional love which cannot be reserved for those only whom we judge to be worthy of our love.

We recall the words of Jesus in John's gospel: "By this everyone will know that you are my disciples, if you have love for one another" (13:35). In other words, the identifying characteristic of true disciples of Jesus will be that they are loving, caring, forgiving persons. This will be far more significant than such things as blessing oneself or wearing a medal or carrying a rosary. Those are laudable things to do, but they will not make us Christians if we do not love others in a universal and unconditional way.

Then Jesus puts an exclamation point to his teaching when he says: "Be merciful, even as your heavenly Father is merciful." Matthew's gospel spells out the implications of this command: "Love your enemies and pray for those who persecute you, so that you may be children of your Father in heaven; for he makes his sun rise on the evil and on the good, and sends rain on the righteous and on the unrighteous" (5:44-45). In other words, our love must try to imitate the love of God, which comes, not from the merit or attractiveness of the one who is loved, but from the goodness of the one who is loving. When we try to love in this divine way, God will join us and enable us to do more than would normally be possible.

When we grow older we need to hear this more than ever.

For we have been around long enough to have been hurt or neglected or perhaps even abused in one way or another. Most of us carry baggage from our past that may include a relationship that has become strained or broken. It is only too true that we hear ourselves saying at times, "Oh, we don't talk anymore," or, "I don't know whether I could ever forgive him or her." When Jesus says that we must forgive, it does not mean that we must say that we were wrong, (though we should be careful not to rule that out completely). But it does mean that we must do our best to be open to reconciliation and to be ready to forgive whatever wrong we may have suffered. Life is simply too short to be wasted on clinging to old hurts.

The reason that this is so important is clear from the words that follow the command to forgive, namely, "and you will be forgiven." Others may have wronged us in one way or another, but we are usually not without blame ourselves. And so we hope that God will "forgive us our trespasses, as we forgive those who trespass against us." The hard truth is that God will be able to show toward us only the degree of mercy that we show toward others.

On the other hand, if we truly forgive others, we can expect to be overwhelmed by the goodness of God "good measure, pressed down, shaken together, running over." Surely we do not want to risk missing such an abundance of divine love and mercy because we still hang on to some long gone injury. What a pity that would be.

69

LIVING THE MEANING OF THE EUCHARIST

While they were eating, (Jesus) took a loaf of bread, and after blessing it he broke it, gave it to (his disciples), and said, "Take; this is my body." Then he took a cup, and after giving thanks he gave it to them, and all of them drank from it. He said to them, "This is my blood of the covenant, which is poured out for many. Truly I tell you, I will never again drink of the fruit of the vine until that day when I drink it new in the kingdom of God" (Mark 14:22-25).

Before the drama of Jesus' passion begins in the Garden of Gethsemane, he has a last meal with his disciples. They have celebrated the Passover meal with him before and they know the ritual well. There is nothing unusual about the fact that he, as the leader of the group, takes the loaf of bread, lifts it up in a gesture of thanksgiving to God, and then breaks it and passes the morsels to them. He does the same with the cup of wine.

However, on this occasion he does something that he has never done before. He sums up for them all that he has been trying to teach them by interpreting the broken bread as his own body and the poured out wine as his own blood. By this profound symbolic gesture, he reveals to them the essence of his whole life, indeed of his very being. He is himself "broken bread" and "poured out wine" because he has offered his life for them and this becomes henceforth their primary spiritual nourishment.

When I say that this was a profoundly "symbolic" gesture, it does not in any way lessen the reality of the presence of Jesus in that Eucharistic bread and wine. When we recognize both the real and symbolic meaning of this central sacrament, we acknowledge also that, in order to benefit from eating the Body of the Lord, we must ourselves become "broken bread" and "poured out blood" through our commitment to unselfish love.

I like to illustrate this important fact through a scenario that one might imagine in my own experience of life in a Benedictine monastery. Let us suppose that a new novice wants very much to be a saint, and as soon as possible. Therefore, instead of attending recreation with the other novices, who are boring at times, he decides to visit the Blessed Sacrament. The amazing thing is that Jesus does not suddenly open the door of the tabernacle and say to this novice, "I appreciate your coming here and by all means do it some other time. But this is the time for you to 'break your body' by joining your brothers in recreation. Please do not use me as an excuse for evading your responsibility of love for others!"

Thus, the breaking of the bread of Jesus' body and the pouring out of the wine of his life-blood do not have some kind of magical power that will save us in spite of ourselves. Rather, they tell us of the extent of Jesus' self-giving for us and will assist us in our own efforts to be loving and generous and forgiving people. That becomes even clearer when we note that Jesus says that his life-blood is his "blood of the covenant." For this means that his sacrificial blood has the binding power of the blood offered to seal the special relationship of God with Israel. To participate in this blood offering is to commit oneself in the most serious way to a life of loving concern for others.

All of this has very important implications for those of us who are growing older. The aging process may very well rob us of the physical and psychic strength that we once had and may therefore limit the kind of work that we can do. However, it does not prevent us from being people who really care about others and who are willing to support them and encourage them in every way possible. There are so many ways in which one can show love that have nothing to do with strength or even good health.

One of the ways in which we older folks can be of great service to others is to make time for them. In our modern society, where "time is money," many feel neglected. This is especially true of children. In the old days, when grandparents often lived with a son or daughter, they were a loving presence in those young lives and filled in the gaps, as it were, when the parents were so busy elsewhere.

This kind of arrangement is rarely possible nowadays but that does not mean that we cannot be creative in finding ways to offer quality time and attentive ears to those who feel unheard and unheeded. Many times it is other older people who need to be heard. No one likes to think that what they have to say is unimportant. Maybe they do repeat their stories but what better way is there to "break one's body" and "pour out one's blood" for others? If we are able to render this loving service, we too will be able to say with Jesus: "I will never again drink of the fruit of the vine until I drink it new in the kingdom of God."

70

BEING STILL BEFORE THE LORD

For with you is the fountain of life…(Psalm 36:9). *Be still before the LORD, and wait patiently for him…. But those who wait for the LORD shall inherit the land* (Psalm 37:7, 9).

It is certainly true that we human beings cherish life beyond any other possession. It is also true that life can become so burdensome, through illness or depression, that we might wonder whether death would not be preferable. However, that would certainly be a very exceptional or temporary situation. In desperate situations, we are usually quite prepared to abandon our most precious material possessions in order to save our lives.

Accordingly, we have attempted throughout history to find a "fountain of youth," that is, a resource that would enable us to prolong our lives and postpone our deaths. Surely there must be somewhere an elixir or potion that will enable us to conquer disease and to ensure good health for the indefinite future. We might even bring our complaint to God with the question: "Why did you give us such a thirst for life and yet made us so unable to avoid death?"

The psalmist cuts off all such fruitless considerations with a simple and definite solution to this human dilemma, as he says to the Lord: "…with you is the fountain of life." Yes, there is indeed an inexhaustible source of life for us, but it exists in the providence of God and lies beyond the life that we now possess. Moreover, in light of God's goodness and love, we can be sure that it is better by far than the life that we know in this world. Even the most vibrant life here must be feeble and shadowy compared to the life that God has in store for us.

In this context, we recall the stirring words of Paul when he declares that "no eye has seen, nor ear heard, nor the human heart conceived, what God has prepared for those who love him" (1Cor 2:9). We are all aware of the folksy wisdom that "a bird in the hand is worth two in the bush," but it is awfully good to know that God has promised that the two birds in the bush can also be ours! And when we receive this double prize, we will be glad to relinquish the one bird we tried so hard to capture.

Then the psalmist offers us exquisite wisdom as he tells us, "Be still before the LORD and wait patiently for him." In other words, we are urged to put aside our impatience, fretfulness and fear and to replace them with calm confidence. For this is what we should expect from those who have experienced the goodness of God and who can afford to wait, patiently and hopefully, for the fulfillment of God's promise of future life for all who trust him and await his happy surprise.

When the psalmist continues, "but those who wait for the LORD shall inherit the land," he is using even more graphic language to assure us that what the Lord has in store for those who love him is well worth waiting for. We modern Americans are so mobile that it is hard for us to imagine the attachment of an Israelite to the land of his ancestors. This was the place of security and the source of life-giving food. It connoted everything that we mean by home—a place where we are welcome and fed and regaled in the midst of a loving family. God promises just such an experience, beyond the uncertainty and finality of this present life, for all who love him and can therefore afford to wait calmly for his gift of eternal life.

Waiting for the Lord is more than just killing time and hoping for the best. It is a very positive attitude that requires deliberate personal decisions. To wait for the Lord is to be still and calm and trusting. In other words, it means to be a truly prayerful person. In prayer we entertain or make room for the presence of God. Without that sense of God's presence it is clearly impossible to be quiet, calm and cheerful. Without that awareness of God's love for us, we will inevitably slip into a state of anxiety and agitated fretfulness. We need to listen carefully then to the words of the psalmist and "be still" as we "wait for the Lord."

Such spiritual stillness is also a great blessing for those who are around us. Truly prayerful people create a zone or an aura that touches all who come near to them. One of the most precious blessings that we can offer others is to bring the gifts of peace and confidence into their lives. And when we focus on helping others in this way, our own quiet confidence grows ever stronger. Our lives can easily become chaotic, and never more so than when we reach our later years. That is why it is so important to have a calm, quiet center where we can always find God and where we can enjoy that rich experience that the Bible calls "shalom," that is, peace.

71

THE END OF THE WORLD IS
THE BEGINNING OF HEAVEN

*There will be signs in the sun, the moon, and the stars, and
on the earth distress among nations confused by the roaring of
the sea and the waves. People will faint from fear and foreboding
of what is coming upon the world, for the powers of the heavens
will be shaken. Then they will see 'the Son of Man coming in
a cloud' with power and great glory. Now when these things
begin to take place, stand up and raise your heads, because
your redemption is drawing near* (Luke 21:25-28).

Most of us would never be tempted to choose such an end-
of-the-world passage as our favorite biblical text. Such a scenario seems so frightening and threatening that we would prefer
to ignore it entirely. As is so often the case, however, a careful
reading of the text provides a far different kind of experience.
After all, we note that the passage ends with some very hopeful
words: we are told to raise our heads, because our redemption
is drawing near! This would be translated today into something
like the civil rights movement's exclamation: "Free at last! Thank
God almighty, free at last!"

The problem is that we are so mesmerized by the description of stars falling from the sky, and the sun and moon being dimmed, that we fail to notice that this end of one world is really the beginning of another and better world. It is true that the world that we see ending is "our world" and we want to cling to what is familiar to us. We fear the unknown. But God is telling us in these apocalyptic images that the unknown world to which he is calling us is far better than any world that we have ever known. The real challenge is, therefore, our need to trust the promises of God. If we can do that, we will be able to let go of a transitory and outmoded world so that a better world can come into being.

I have often thought that our problem with the end of this world is somewhat like the situation of an infant in its mother's womb. Being born out of that warm and secure place into the cold outer world must be a very traumatic experience for such an infant. I suspect that, if that infant were given an option, it might very well choose to stay in the womb. But we know that this would be a tragic choice, for the child would then never come to know the opportunities and joys of independent existence. Worse than that, its choice would lead to death for both itself and its mother.

We too are in the womb of our present life. We may have had trials and tribulations here as well as victories and joys. But we still want to hang on to what we know and we want to stay with the people who have been an important part of this life. Nonetheless, it is clear that, from God's perspective, it would be a terrible tragedy to cling to this "half-life" and to miss the fullness of life that God has in store for his faithful ones.

If we stop to think about it, we realize that we have been dealing with the ends of many worlds in our lives. There is the end of childhood with its carefree atmosphere, and the end of our education with our final graduation, and the end of our busy but rewarding life with children as we try to cope with the "empty-nest" experience, and the end of our working life as we retire from full-time employment. All of these ends can be difficult but we know that life goes on and that the new life that comes has its blessings also.

How we handle all these preliminary endings will tell us a lot about how gracefully we will be able to deal with the ultimate ending on this earth. It is interesting to note that when the Bible tells us that the end of the world will be announced with cosmic disturbances, such as, the falling of stars and the dimming of the light of the sun and moon, it is actually telling us about similar phenomena that often accompany our own experience of aging. The sun and the moon were the "clocks" of the ancient, biblical world. They were the ultimate examples of regularity and stability. As we approach the end of this temporary existence, we may very well begin to have difficulty remembering what time it is. I recall seeing in a home for the aged a large sign on the bulletin board saying: The next meal is lunch! This means that our own "sun and moon and stars" are no longer reliable signposts to help us organize our days. But we can accept these signs of our human condition with grace and dignity if we also know with a vibrant sense of faith that there is, not just lunch, but a real feast awaiting us in the kingdom of God.

72

WITH GOD WE CAN WORK MIRACLES

When it was evening, the disciples came to (Jesus) and said, "This is a deserted place, and the hour is now late; send the crowds away so that they may go into the villages and buy food for themselves." Jesus said to them, "They need not go away; you give them something to eat." They replied, "We have nothing here but five loaves and two fish." And he said, "Bring them here to me...." Taking the five loaves and the two fish, he looked up to heaven and blessed and broke the loaves, and gave them to the disciples, and the disciples gave them to the crowds. And all ate and were filled; and they took up what was left over of the broken pieces, twelve baskets full (Matt 14:15-18, 19b-20).

The miracle of the multiplication of loaves and fish is so important for the gospel writers that we find no less than five accounts of this story (two of them in Matthew's gospel). We need to pay special attention, therefore, to a miracle that is so central to the meaning of Jesus' mission of salvation.

The story line is quite simple and straightforward. A dilemma has been created by the appearance of a large crowd of people who have followed Jesus into a deserted area and who now have no means of acquiring food to satisfy their hunger. Jesus then, in an almost casual manner, tells his disciples to find food for the multitude. They can scarcely believe what they hear from him. His command is so preposterous that they are dumbfounded.

The disciples do point out that they have five loaves of bread and two fish. This is no doubt intended for their own small meal. And so they note what must be obvious: that this meager supply is so inadequate as to be almost a mockery of their best intentions. In John's version of the miracle, their words name the problem most eloquently: "But what are they (the loaves and fish) among so many people (6:9)?"

In many ways, this statement is a perfect summary of the human side of the story. It includes all those thousand and one situations when we know that something needs to be done but have no idea how we can respond effectively in view of our totally inadequate resources. We may desperately seek to promote peace in the world or, at least, to reduce in some way the violence that we see among nations, in communities and in families. But we feel frustrated by our apparent total lack of ability to address these problems in any meaningful way.

We must notice that Jesus does not respond to the expressed helplessness of the disciples by saying, "Oh, I hadn't noticed that you were so short of food." Rather, he asks them to see this as a joint venture of both them and himself. He tells them, "Bring them (the meager rations) here to me." It would be a serious mistake to pass over this seemingly innocent command. In fact, we can paraphrase the words of Jesus as follows, "Include me in your plans and you will no longer have to accept helplessness as your only recourse in this dilemma."

We will include God in our plans by making him a part

of every decision in our lives. This means that we will never approach any problem without first acknowledging our dependence on God's goodness and mercy. We do this in regular and personal prayer. And in this prayer we ask God to stir up our imaginations so that we will be able to think of better ways to attack the problems we see in our society.

If we are getting on in years, we will ask God to give us the wonderful gift of hope so that we do not succumb to a feeling of uselessness or helplessness. When the lad, David, offered to fight the giant, Goliath, he was inspired by God to think of a new way to deal with this seemingly hopeless situation. Thus his God-assisted imagination led him to think of the sling as the new and better weapon. And when he did so, the giant was suddenly as good as dead. I heard it said once that Saul and his men looked at Goliath and said, "How big he is; how can we fight him?" But David looked at the same giant and said, "How big he is; how can I miss him!"

The giant that confronts those of us who seem to have seen our best years is the fear of illness and loss of control. If we rely only on our own resources we will find it impossible to confront this "giant." It is at such times that we will need to hear what Jesus said to the apparently helpless disciples, "Bring (your problems) here to me." And then we will also be able to share the amazement of the disciples as Jesus takes our poverty and makes it the source of extraordinary riches: "And all ate and were filled; and they took up what was left over of the broken pieces, twelve baskets full."

73

IN GOD I TRUST, I AM NOT AFRAID

In you our ancestors trusted; they trusted and you delivered them. To you they cried, and were saved; in you they trusted, and were not put to shame (Ps 22:4-5). Then my enemies will retreat in the day when I call. This I know, that God is for me.... in God I trust; I am not afraid.... My vows to you I must perform, O God; I will render thank offerings to you. For you have delivered my soul from death, and my feet from falling, so that I may walk before God in the light of life (Ps 56:9, 11-13).

Trusting another person is an act of free will that is as difficult as it is beneficial. Most transactions in our everyday lives, from writing checks to giving out our credit card number, are largely based on trust. Sometimes this trust is abused and we feel betrayed. Indeed, if this happens too often, we may adopt a defensive mode and become so cautious that we miss much of the joy that life can offer. It is a terrible experience to feel that no one can be trusted.

Trusting others in business affairs is important but it cannot compare with trusting that involves our very lives. We must trust doctors to whom we turn for life-giving surgery. We ask God to guide their fingers so that they will be able to find all the cancer or may make this by-pass the best they have ever done. Fortunately, our trust is usually rewarded by competent, and sometimes exceptional, intervention.

But what about the trust that we must try to find when all human resources are exhausted? Ultimately, it is only God whom we can trust to rescue us from despair or from the apparent finality of death. Nothing in this whole world is more important than the ability to trust God when no one else is able to help us.

The psalmist understood this perfectly and it is a constant refrain in many of the psalms. It is important to approach this matter as the psalmist does, first of all by recalling the example of his ancestors. We owe so much to those who have gone before us, and nothing they have done for us is more important than their example of loving trust in God. We have seen how our parents or grandparents have usually faced death with a child-like trust in God that was nothing less than inspiring. This doesn't suggest that it was easy for them, but when the time came they could draw upon the presence of the God whom they had honored all their lives for reassurance and comfort.

We recall that Psalm twenty-two is the one that Jesus turned to in the last moments of his death on the cross: "My God, my God, why have you forsaken me" (v. 1)? This verse may sound like a cry of despair, but it is only the beginning of the psalm. The later verses are all about trusting God, and at the end the psalmist can say: "For he did not despise or abhor the affliction of the afflicted; he did not hide his face from me, but heard when I cried to him" (v. 24). We will never need more trust than Jesus did at the hour of his death.

We need to pray every day that we will be able to say with

the psalmist: "This I know, that God is for me." One does not know that from reading books or listening to lectures. These may help, but such conviction comes only from the gift of faith…and growth in faith comes only from deeply personal prayer. Such prayer would be, for example, the last words of the "Our Father," where we say, at Jesus' request, "And do not bring us to the time of trial, but rescue us from the evil one" (Matt 6:13). In other words, we ask God to be with us at the end when we are most vulnerable to despair.

Having said those words with the confidence that comes from knowing that Jesus has asked us to do so, we can again say with the psalmist those blessed words: "I am not afraid." This is not the defiant cry of the atheist who refuses to trust and may even arrange his own death. Rather, it is the far wiser sentiment of one who is glad to be a creature and to accept life, from beginning to end, from a gracious and merciful God.

Then the psalmist thanks God for the deliverance that is yet to come. This often happens in the Psalms and it is a beautiful example of the psalmist's trust in God's goodness. It is like saying, "I am so sure of your favorable response that I want to thank you in advance."

The outcome of God's response to sincere trust is expressed in words that we all would like to make our own: "For you have delivered my soul from death, and my feet from falling, so that I may walk before God in the light of life." This is the final victory of light over darkness; this is our participation in the resurrection of Jesus. And so our trust is vindicated and our hopes are fulfilled. Amen! So be it!

74

TRUSTING GOD AT THE END

*They went to a place called Gethsemane; and (Jesus) said
to his disciples, "Sit here while I pray." He took with him Peter
and James and John, and began to be distressed and agitated.
And he said to them, "I am deeply grieved, even to death;
remain here, and keep awake." And going a little farther, he
threw himself on the ground and prayed that, if it were possible,
the hour might pass from him. He said, "Abba, Father, for you
all things are possible; remove this cup from me; yet, not what
I want, but what you want" (Mark 14:32-36).*

After studying and teaching the gospels over many years, I
am convinced that, just as the passion story is the most important part of each gospel, so also is the "agony in the garden" the
central event in the passion story. We may be inclined to think
that Jesus' death on the cross is surely the climax of the passion
story. However, if we think the matter through, I believe that we
will agree that the most important moment in dying is not the
moment of death itself but the critical moment when we agree
to die. And this is what Jesus did in the garden of Gethsemane.

In Mark's version, the author wants us to understand first

of all that Jesus is entering into a more personal and private moment in his life. He indicates this by showing how Jesus left most of his disciples and took with him only three—Peter, James and John—who were his most intimate companions. (We recall that they alone accompanied him to the mount of the Transfiguration).

Jesus had prayed with his disciples many times before in the garden of Gethsemane. That is why Judas knew exactly where to find him. But the disciples had never seen him in such distress as he is now. He knows that his death is imminent. We may prepare ourselves for dying but the last twenty-four hours are not like any other day in our lives.

We may wonder how the Son of God could be so distressed in the face of death, but the fact is that he is also a human being. My New Testament professor in Jerusalem told us students that there is one conclusion that we must avoid at all cost and that is that Jesus was only pretending to be afraid of death. In fact, he wanted to share our lives in every way except sin. And that surely includes the difficult experience of dying.

Jesus then told Peter, James and John to remain there as he went deeper still into the garden, now completely alone. His physical movement is not nearly as important as is his psychological progression. He is now confronting his imminent death and this can only be done alone. We hope that we will have friends around us when we die, but the fact is that we always die alone…unless we know and love God!

Jesus does know and love his heavenly Father. And so he asks him most earnestly whether it might not be possible to change the script of his messianic mission. I think he is asking only for a postponement. He might have said, "Father, I know that I must die at Passover time, but why could it not be next year?" But then he recognizes that this is what his Father wants and so he accepts it without hesitation: "yet, not what I want, but what you want." In effect, he is saying to this loving Father, whom he has come to know and trust: "If this is what you wish for me, I would not have it any other way, not because I understand why it must be so, but because I trust you without reservation".

Those who work in hospices tell us that the decisive moment in dying comes, not at the last breath, but when the patient agrees to die. If we are believers, this means that we, like Jesus, simply agree with God that it is time to go. This is not an easy decision to make but it is a wonderful blessing and a special grace to be able to trust our heavenly Father enough to accept this moment when it comes.

Being able to trust God is the key to dying in a peaceful way. But that is not something that we can postpone until the last moment. Learning to trust God begins many years before it is time to die. This ability is nurtured in regular prayer. Jesus knew and trusted his heavenly Father because, as the gospels tell us, he frequently went aside and prayed, sometimes all night long. And we note that he told his disciples at Gethsemane that they should "Keep awake and pray…" (Mark 14:38).

While we still have time then, we should make room for God in our lives by regular and fervent prayer. In this way we will establish a deep friendship with God so that, when we come to that last personal and private moment, we will know that God is there with us. Such prayer does not require special words. All we need to do is to be attentive to God and to ask him to make us his friends. Being a friend of God will open the door to eternal life in God's loving presence.

75

STRIVING TO BE BOTH VULNERABLE AND TRUSTING

(Martha) went back and called her sister Mary, and told her privately, "The Teacher is here and is calling for you".... When Jesus saw (Mary) weeping...he was greatly disturbed in spirit and deeply moved. He said, "Where have you laid (Lazarus)?" They said to him, "Lord, come and see." Jesus began to weep (John 11:28, 33-35).

In the story of the raising of Lazarus, Jesus does nothing about the death of his friend until he has discussed the matter, first with Martha, and then with Mary, both of whom were sisters of Lazarus. This seems a bit strange because the story is supposed to be about Lazarus, but he is left waiting in the tomb and when he finally is raised to life he is not given a single word to say! In fact, however, the story is really about how we mortal human beings should relate to Jesus who is the source of true life.

When Jesus talked to Martha, who had rushed out to meet him before he entered the village of Bethany, he ended with a profound theological statement: "I am the resurrection and the life" (John 11:25). This is a very important statement and it has wonderful implications. However, it does not help Lazarus!

Everything changes when we come to Mary. She had remained at home and, when Martha came to her, it is said that she spoke to her "privately." The Greek adverb suggests that she spoke very softly, or perhaps merely whispered. This is a kind of body language by which we are told that Mary is the contemplative one, who does not attack death, but calmly turns it all over to the mercy and goodness of God. She sees death as a mystery to be solved rather than as an enemy to be destroyed.

When she hears that Jesus is calling for her, she quickly responds and goes to meet him. Then something very strange happens. Jesus does not give her a theological statement, as he did with Martha, but instead is deeply moved himself. The Greek verb is very strong and suggests a mixture of anger and concern. There is something about Mary that causes Jesus to respond in a profoundly personal way. Not only that, but he immediately moves into action and wants to know where Lazarus is buried. He wants to challenge death because it has caused such grief among his friends…and because he himself is a friend of Lazarus.

When the bystanders respond, "Lord, come and see," it is like an echo of that other occasion when Jesus told two disciples who had followed him, "Come and see," with the promise of real life (John 1:39). We, like the people in this story, can only point to the graveyard as the outcome of our lives. But Jesus wants to show us a new life that extends far beyond the apparent end represented by the cemetery.

It is important for us to know what exactly it was about the attitude of Mary that caused this deeply personal and effective reaction on the part of Jesus. This is important because we very much want to have Jesus react in the same way in our own struggle with the power of death, whether among our friends or in our own experience. I think that the attitude of Mary is a wonderful combination of vulnerability and trust.

When we are dealing with God, we need to put aside our deep yearning for control, which is often manifested in a bravado that is totally out of place. We are only creatures, and we should not be ashamed to admit our dependence on the goodness of our Creator. Then we must adopt an attitude of trust, which means that we rely on our faith conviction about the love and goodness of God. Our dying becomes in fact the last and best opportunity we will ever have to trust God. It is truly the victory of faith over history!

The readiness of God to respond to our trust in him is expressed most forcefully in the reaction of Jesus to the tears of Mary: "Jesus began to weep." This show of emotion is especially surprising in John's gospel where Jesus seems to be in charge at all times. It also shows us that God can truly feel our grief and is more than ready to help us. When all the tears are wiped away, we will see and understand this consistent and ultimately victorious love of God over every obstacle.

The most important lesson to take from this story of Mary's quiet confidence before the mystery of death is that we too should strive to accept our own vulnerability and should learn to trust the wisdom of God in these difficult times of our lives. The feeling of being unprotected from hurt is especially common among those of us who are getting on in years. All the more reason then to beg God to give us the ability to trust his goodness and to look forward to the victory of life that he has promised us.

76

WALKING HUMBLY WITH OUR GOD

With what shall I come before the LORD, and bow myself before God on high? Shall I come before him with burnt offerings, with calves a year old? Will the LORD be pleased with thousands of rams, with ten thousands of rivers of oil?…. He has told you, O mortal, what is good; and what does the LORD require of you but to do justice, and to love kindness, and to walk humbly with your God (Mic 6:6-8)?

As we get on in years, we must inevitably think about what we have accomplished in our lives. In most cases, we will be able to recall the children we have raised, the contributions we have made to our town or to society in general, the degrees we have earned and the awards we may have won. And then we will wonder how much all this will stand up to the scrutiny of God in that last judgment. For we have certainly passed up many opportunities for doing good and we may have shameful things in our past that we regret. We have done many things to please ourselves or others, but how much of this will be pleasing to God?

The prophet Micah deals directly with this problem and his

words can help us to evaluate our own standing before God as we approach the final assessment of our lives. "With what shall I come before the LORD?" How will we answer the searching questions of God about our response to the opportunity that life has provided for us? Above all, have God's presence and wisdom been at the center of our lives, or have they been honored only at times of convenience or when we felt threatened?

In dealing with these questions, the prophet recognizes that he has been a religious person as far as the external signs of religion are concerned. He has been careful to offer to God all the prescribed sacrifices. His public show of religion has been commendable. But he realizes that this kind of external religious observance can never be enough. The offering of calves and rams and oil, even in extravagant numbers or amounts, are important only as external signs of a deeper offering of our love of God and attention to his presence in our lives.

Micah reminds us that, if we pay attention to God's word, it will be clear that religion must be deeply personal and not just an external show: "He has told you, O mortal, what is good." The fact that we are addressed here as "mortals" reminds us of our radical weakness and warns us that we will never be able to survive our mortality and find a new kind of life without paying close attention to the deeper and more personal demands of religion.

What is it then that God will require of us when the whole truth is finally brought to light? The answer is found in a text that is one of the most simple and most beautiful statements in the entire Bible. "And what does God require of you but to do justice, and to love kindness, and to walk humbly with your God?" If we can respond positively to these questions, we will surely be delivered from the darkness of death and be brought into the eternal light that God has reserved for those who have found him and have honored his words.

To "do justice" means more than just to be honest in one's business affairs or to pay one's debts, although that is surely included. It means to be a good person—one who is sensitive to the needs of others and who represents, as much as possible, the presence of Jesus in this world. This does not imply some kind of heroic behavior. Rather, it asks us about our everyday activities: Have we smiled, and thanked, and forgiven, and remembered? In a word, have we "loved kindness?"

To be a kind person is to be thoughtful and considerate. It is to make Paul's description of Christian love an ideal for our lives: "Love is patient; love is kind; love is not envious or boastful or arrogant or rude. It does not insist on its own way; it is not irritable or resentful; it does not rejoice in wrongdoing, but rejoices in the truth" (1 Cor 13:4-6). We will notice that, in this wonderful description of love, there is nothing romantic or lyrical. There is nothing wrong with being romantic and lyrical, but first of all, we must be kind and thoughtful.

Finally, we are told that we must "walk humbly" with our God. This does not mean that we must walk around all day with our heads down or that our attitude toward God should be one of fear. But it does mean that we must always remember how much we need God and how grateful we should be for his goodness to us. And when we learn how to walk humbly with God, we will also know how to be patient and forgiving and gentle toward all our fellow humans.

77

ACQUIRING A CHILD-LIKE SENSE OF WONDER

At that time the disciples came to Jesus and asked, "Who is the greatest in the kingdom of heaven?" He called a child, whom he put among them, and said, "Truly I tell you, unless you change and become like children, you will never enter the kingdom of heaven. Whoever becomes humble like this child is the greatest in the kingdom of heaven. Whoever welcomes one such child in my name welcomes me" (Matt 18:1-5).

We can easily relate to the disciples of Jesus in this scene because they are so much like the rest of us. They want immediate and tangible results from their friendship with the Master—a Master who has demonstrated his ability to make things happen. When he talks about the kingdom of heaven, they are not interested in a kingdom that will come in some future age; they want a political kingdom, here and now, and they fully expect to hold positions of power and honor in that kingdom. We recall how Jesus caught them arguing among themselves about who was "the greatest," meaning no doubt, who would hold the choice cabinet positions in the new regime (Mark 9:34)!

Jesus does not attempt to argue with them or even to scold

them. Rather, he performs a simple action that has profound symbolic implications. He calls a child that was standing or playing nearby and asks that child to stand in the middle of their little circle. Then he turns to his disciples and makes a statement that is so challenging that even today we can scarcely grasp all its implications.

"Unless you change and become like children, you will never enter the kingdom of heaven." First of all, they need to change. They need to put aside their yearnings for prestige and power in this world and to begin to look for a kingdom that is far better and far more lasting. How can they do that? It will happen when they "become like children!"

It is of great importance that we understand what Jesus means because what he is saying about becoming like children applies to us also. We may be inclined to think that Jesus means that we should be as innocent as little children. But surely that cannot be the meaning, for then it is much too late for most of us. We may not be public sinners, but we surely have lost the simple innocence that we associate with little children.

I am convinced that Jesus means that we must discover once again the sense of wonder that is typical of normal and healthy little children. For they have not yet been infected with the adult virus of cynicism. We tend to become suspicious and cynical because we are often disappointed in our search for happiness. People may have betrayed us, or events may have turned against us. And so we are tempted to distrust life and to become much more cautious than we should be. We warn our children about talking to strangers or about believing in everything they hear. This is good advice because the world is full of danger. The great danger in this defensive attitude is, however, that it can also affect our relationship with God. For God too is in many ways a stranger to us. He is so powerful and so distant, it seems, and his ways are so mysterious.

When Jesus says that we must become like little children, therefore, he is asking us to trust the incredible promises of God, just as little children will be ready to believe the wild tales of a doting grandparent. They are a wonderfully receptive audience for someone who wants to spin tales of exaggerated adventures "once upon a time!"

The promises of God are not exaggerated stories, however. On the contrary, they are so wonderful and so trustworthy that even a childlike imagination cannot fully appreciate them. In dealing with God's promises, the problem is not with the wonder of the promises but with our ability to comprehend them. Paul understood this very well, for he wrote to the Corinthians, "What no eye has seen, nor ear heard, nor the human heart conceived, what God has prepared for those who love him" (1 Cor 2:9).

Sometimes we hear people refer to old age as a second childhood. That is usually understood in a negative sense, suggesting that old people become irresponsible or naïve. But there is a wonderful way in which that may be true. For older people can also acquire the sense of wonder that Jesus extols. Looking toward the future with divinely inspired hope, they can become like little children looking forward to Christmas or a birthday party. Nothing could contradict the tired pessimism of the world in which we live more than such a beautiful witness to the validity of God's precious promises. "Unless you become like little children...."

78

DISCOVERING A NEW LIFE IN JESUS

A Samaritan woman came to draw water, and Jesus said to her, "Give me a drink"…. The Samaritan woman said to him, "How is it that you, a Jew, ask a drink of me, a woman of Samaria…?" Jesus answered her, "If you knew the gift of God, and who it is that is saying to you, 'Give me a drink,' you would have asked him, and he would have given you living water…. Everyone who drinks of this water will be thirsty again, but those who drink of the water that I will give them will never be thirsty. The water that I will give will become in them a spring of water gushing up to eternal life" (John 4:7, 9-10, 13-14).

This story of how Jesus met a Samaritan woman and asked her for a drink is delightful in its own right. But it is also a powerfully symbolic story, which has much to tell us about our own lives and about our quest for eternal happiness. The woman is at first surprised that Jesus would ask her for a drink since Jewish men were never supposed to talk to an adult woman in public. Moreover, as a Samaritan, she belonged to a people who were generally despised by the Jews because they had inter-married with non-Jewish persons during the Exile and were considered only half Jews.

Jesus does not answer her question but leads her instead to another level of meaning as he offers her "living water." She has been surviving under the burden of a kind of social invisibility; she knows what it means to be ignored. In effect, she says to Jesus, "Don't you know about those rules that reduce me to being a nobody?" But Jesus knows all about those terrible rules, and he has come to invalidate them. He offers her instead the living water of spiritual birth.

There is no comparison between the stale well water (her condition of bondage) and the living, spring water that Jesus offers (a new vision of life through faith in him as Savior). People who try to survive on well water will only get thirsty again but the new water of faith that Jesus offers is like a spring of fresh, cold water that gushes out of the earth in such profusion that one never has to look for water again.

When I was a young boy, I fell ill with pneumonia. This was before antibiotics and I was being treated with mustard poultices. It was summertime and my fever, plus the summer heat, made me yearn for the water from a spring that was at the lower end of our farm. I told my Dad that I thought I would feel better if I could just have a drink from that spring. He felt so helpless that he was glad to be able to do anything, so he hurried to bring some water from that spring. It was not very cold by the time it reached me, but it was so refreshing, because it was such a wonderful sign of my father's love and concern. This has always helped me to understand a bit better what Jesus is talking about in this story.

It is not so hard for us to identify, at least at times, with that Samaritan woman. This is especially true when we grow older. We feel unappreciated and hardly even noticed by all the young people who are so busy and so preoccupied with the affairs of their own lives. Scarcely anyone seems to remember how hard we have worked and how many sacrifices we have made. Sometimes we are even tempted to wonder whether we should not just quietly disappear.

But Jesus says to us, as he said to that neglected Samaritan woman: I have a vision of life that can make all the difference for you. If you will just trust the message that I bring to you, you will know how precious you are in the eyes of God. And then you will find it easier to understand why other people seem not to care as much as we would like. In fact, we might then be free enough to admit that we acted pretty much in the same way when we were young and were so busy about many things.

I sometimes think that this is the point of the miracle of Cana as well. In a symbolic sense, the jars full of water represent our own lives without faith in the goodness of God. We are alive but life doesn't seem very interesting. Then Jesus asks us to look again, but this time with the eyes of faith. Suddenly the jars are full of sparkling, colorful wine. For it is true that faith can illuminate the landscape of our lives so that a life that seemed dull and uninteresting can become bright and filled with flowers!

This may seem to be a miracle but it really can come to pass. And it is such a beautiful thing to see in those who are getting on in years and are tempted to believe that there is not much left for them. No matter how old we may be, we can become such a blessing in the lives of others as we share with them the "living water" that Jesus has given to us and that can be so wonderfully refreshing.

79

FINDING RELEASE FROM BONDAGE

For you, O God, have tested us; you have tried us as silver is tried. You brought us into the net; you laid burdens on our backs; you let people ride over our heads; we went through fire and through water; yet you have brought us out to a spacious place (Ps 66:10-12).

Anyone who has lived fifty or more years on this earth will not need to ask what the psalmist means when he says, "For you, O God, have tested us; you have tried us as silver is tried." I can easily remember the day on which I made my solemn vows as a Benedictine monk. My family was there and they seemed to be saying, "Have you really given up everything for the kingdom of God?" And I seemed to suggest to them, "Oh yes! Everything!" Little did I realize how naïve I was about what life would actually bring and about how difficult it would be to live the generosity that I had pledged to God.

I am sure that this is not an uncommon experience in human life. How could a newly married couple possibly know what hardships lie ahead and how much they may have to learn about sharing and being patient and adapting to all kinds of challenges? And yet we would hardly ever say that our youthful pledges were mistakes. Indeed, in our calmer moments, we would be ready and willing to do it all again.

The psalmist pictures God as the one who has given us these trials and challenges, but that is true only in the sense that God has given us this human life where such hardships are inevitable. Moreover, this "trial by fire" is also an opportunity to grow and mature and become a better, more generous person. It is for that reason that the psalmist says that we are tried "as silver is tried." Silver is not found in a pure state. It must be brought to a level of intense heat so that the dross can be removed. But it is so much more precious after it has been subjected to this "ordeal." Looking back, we too know that we are usually better and stronger and more tolerant persons from having endured hardships in life.

It is interesting to note the imagery used by the psalmist in describing the nature of these challenges. He pictures us as constrained or bound or confined to a narrow place. We are caught in a net, or weighed down by a heavy burden or feel that people are running roughshod over us. We may even have to "go through fire and water." All of these vivid images suggest that we are cramped or choked or imprisoned in some way.

I think it is pretty obvious that these images are very appropriate for those of us who are getting on in years. We may not feel free to make a long journey because we fear becoming ill in a foreign country. Or we may find that we must depend on others to get to the supermarket. When our age begins to take a greater toll, we may be confined to our homes, or to our rooms and finally to our beds. The world seems to be closing in around us. We yearn for the time when we will once again be able to breathe deeply and run and play as we did in childhood.

It is exactly this dream of wide-open spaces that the psalmist promises to those who trust in the goodness of God: "You have brought us out to a spacious place." We cannot even imagine how spacious that place will really be. "No eye has seen, nor ear heard, nor the human heart conceived, what God has prepared for those who love him" (1 Cor 2:9). The walls that now seem to box us in will be dissolved and we will once again be free and full of energy…and grateful to the God who has brought us to this blessed place.

This sense of being trapped or imprisoned is expressed also in the well-known Psalm 130. In this case, we feel that we are in some deep, dark pit and that escape is quite impossible. We cry out to God for help: "Out of the depths I cry to you, O LORD. LORD, hear my voice (v. 1)." We fear that our rescue is impossible, but we have learned to trust in God. Once again, we hear the psalmist assure us that God will hear our prayer. "For with the LORD there is steadfast love, and with him is great power to redeem (v. 7)." The psalmist assures us that it is only a matter of time until God will reach down and pull us out of that pit and take us into his strong arms where we will be safe forever.

Feeling trapped is a terrible experience but it can be tolerated if we can see a way out of our bondage. The Bible tells us in the clearest terms that God is this way out of every dilemma. Praise the LORD for his goodness to us! "With him there is great power to redeem" (Ps 130:7).

80

THE FAITH THAT CONQUERS DEATH

Then Jesus said to the Jews who had believed in him, "If you continue in my word, you are truly my disciples; and you will know the truth, and the truth will make you free.... Very truly, I tell you, whoever keeps my word will never see death" (John 8:31-32, 51).

It is probably safe to say that everyone wants to be free— free of worry and fear and guilt. Every time we think of something we would like to do, there is that nagging concern that it won't work out or will be too dangerous or will eat up too much of our savings. If we could only be free to follow our dreams, without concern or worry about anything! It is for that reason, I think, that this passage from John's gospel is so appealing to most of us.

Jesus had been talking to some Jews about how he has a mission from the Father to bring salvation to the world. They were naturally interested in what he is saying and they "believed in him." However, it soon becomes evident that their faith is only tentative. For Jesus asks them to "continue in my word." The Greek verb that is translated here as "continue" is the same one that elsewhere is translated as "abide." This clearly implies that Jesus wants them to grow in their faith and to allow that faith to penetrate their defenses and to change, gradually but surely, their whole way of looking at life.

It is only when this happens that they will be truly his disciples and will "know the truth" that will make them free. Knowing the truth does not mean becoming more educated or reading a new book. This truth, in John's gospel, is the revelation that Jesus brings from his heavenly Father, first of all about the Father's unconditional love for us, and then about our need to respond to that love by loving others. There is no more important truth in the whole world than this revelation of Jesus.

We can now understand in what sense Jesus tells those tentative disciples that "the truth will make you free." As we gradually come to know and to experience the love of God for us, his beloved children, we become more confident and more able to be our true selves and more free from fear and low self-esteem. It is as if the ice of fear that held us in its grip begins to melt and to break up as we are able to rediscover our spontaneity and creativity. Our imaginations are released so that we can dream and plan and even make a few mistakes without losing our confidence.

This teaching of Jesus that the only true freedom comes from converting love received into love given is at the very heart of his wisdom. This is not easy to understand since we often find it hard to receive love because we think that there may be too many strings attached. And we are right in the sense that being loved enables us to love others and that includes an obligation to do so. But if we have the courage to offer our love to others we soon discover to our amazement that we are more free than ever. This can only be because we were created for this purpose and therefore we are fulfilling our destiny and are seizing the most wonderful opportunity that life can offer us.

This wisdom of Jesus is so contrary to the wisdom of the secular society in which we live that we find it difficult to live in that society and still trust the wisdom of Jesus. Secular wisdom tells us to seek success and self-confidence, to be sure, but primarily for the purpose of achieving our own goals, even if that means neglecting or abusing others. The fallacy of this secular wisdom becomes only too evident when we grow older and no longer have the strength to succeed in the world's way. But growing old is no handicap at all if we trust the wisdom of Jesus. For older people can still love and care and forgive…and in many ways they can do this better than when they were young and often preoccupied with succeeding.

There is another great advantage of the wisdom of Jesus over merely human reasoning. Jesus makes this clear when he tells us in the most solemn way, "Very truly, I tell you, whoever keeps my word will never see death." This does not mean that we will not die. Rather, it assures us that, if we live unselfishly and try to be a loving presence in our world, we will acquire a new life that cannot be touched at all by our physical death.

This is expressed most eloquently in the words of Paul, "Death has been swallowed up in victory. Where, O death, is your victory? Where, O death, is your sting" (1 Cor 15:54-55)? Thus, the validation of the wisdom of Jesus comes at the end when it alone leads to immortality and glory. These words of Paul are like music in the ears of those who are beginning to experience the problems of the later years. For they tell us that we may indeed laugh at the inevitability of the aging process as we put all our confidence in the promises of Jesus.

81

Seeing the Humor in Aging

Remember your Creator in the days of your youth, before the bad times come and the years draw near when you will say, "I have no pleasure in them."...Remember him in the day when...those who look through the windows can see no longer, when the street doors are shut, when the sound of the mill fades, when the chirping of the sparrow grows faint and the song-birds fall silent, when people are afraid of a steep place and the street is full of terrors, when the blossom whitens on the almond tree and the locust can only crawl and caper-buds no longer give zest. For mortals depart to their everlasting home, and the mourners go about the street (Eccl 12:1,3-5; Revised English Bible).

In this passage from Ecclesiastes, we discover how realistic the Bible can be when it comes to describing the situation of many older people. This book is well known for its rather pessimistic assessment of human life, as expressed in its opening paragraph: "Vanity of vanities! All is vanity" (1:2). Nonetheless, it provides a necessary corrective to a romantic and sugarcoated description of the realities of old age. A positive and healthy understanding of our later years does not come from denial of reality but rather from a vision of the future beyond this often difficult period of life.

When the author urges us to remember our Creator in the days of youth, he is pointing out that we will never be able to deal with old age unless we think often of the goodness of the God who made us and who, being good and gracious, wants us to find happiness. We need to think of this and make it part of our prayers, not only in youth, since it may be too late for that, but also on those carefree and "youthful" days that may still occur in our later years. In this way, though we may still not "have pleasure" in these years, we will nonetheless keep a healthy and positive attitude.

When the author begins to describe in detail the characteristics of our later years, it is all too easy to recognize ourselves in his word-pictures. And it is important to see also that his descriptions are not lacking in humor. After all, if we can't laugh occasionally at the foibles of old age, we will probably find its burdens unbearable. And the more we trust God, the more we will be able to "lighten up" and see the humor in life.

We are told that "those who look through the windows can see no longer." This is no doubt a reference to the failing eyesight that often plagues us older folks. Our eyes are the windows through which we see the outside world and the author seems to imply that we just can't seem to get them clean any more! The fact that the "street doors are shut" implies that we have become less adventuresome and that we choose, more and more, to stay in the "safe" environment of our houses.

We discover that "the sound of the mill fades" when our teeth are not as good as they used to be. This would have been especially true of the author's time when dental care was virtually non-existent. But we probably realize that, even with good care, our chewing may not be as good as it used to be.

It is not difficult to recognize what is happening "when the chirping of the sparrow grows faint and the song-birds fall silent." Loss of hearing is an almost inevitable experience of the aging process. No doubt the "chirping" of the sparrows is the first sound to be missed since loss of hearing affects especially our ability to pick up the high notes.

We older folks know why we are "afraid of a steep place," because our steps are not as sure as they used to be. The streets too seem more dangerous now, especially in our modern days when we have to cope with speeding automobiles. The white blossoms on the almond tree are a metaphor for the white hair that graces our heads. We tell ourselves that at least we have hair, but we would all prefer to have the natural hair of our youth.

The reference to the locust is problematic since other versions translate this word as "grasshopper," and see it as a reference to the stiff-legged gait of many older folks. (There's humor there too!). The caper buds are still used to enliven bland foods and were once thought to be an aphrodisiac. In either case, they are no longer of much use to us.

The final comments of our author are quite optimistic. For he tells us that there is an "everlasting home" awaiting us, prepared by that loving Creator whose power is able to overcome our obvious weaknesses. If this is true, we need not pay attention to the "mourners," for they grieve only for a temporary life that finally gives way to God's resurrection glory.

82

SO WE DO NOT LOSE HEART

So we do not lose heart. Even though our outer nature is wasting away, our inner nature is being renewed day by day. For this slight momentary affliction is preparing us for an eternal weight of glory beyond all measure, because we look not at what can be seen but at what cannot be seen; for what can be seen is temporary, but what cannot be seen is eternal (2 Cor 4:16-18).

For those of us who are getting on in years, this is indeed a "golden text." There are few if any passages in the entire Bible that express more clearly than these words of Paul the solid hope that will enable us to deal positively with the experience of aging.

First of all, Paul does not attempt to put a sugar coating on the pill that we must all swallow. When he says that our outer nature is wasting away, he makes an observation that is easy to verify if we are beyond sixty or seventy years of age, and we may not even have to wait that long.

Paul gives us an even more graphic illustration of the ravages of aging in his Letter to the Romans, where he describes the elderly condition of Abraham and Sarah. He tells us that "(Abraham) did not weaken in faith when he considered his own body, which was already as good as dead (for he was about a hundred years old), or when he considered the barrenness of Sarah's womb" (4:19).

This does not mean that Abraham spent a lot of time looking at the sad condition of his body or reflecting on the unpromising condition of Sarah's womb. But it does mean that he was fully aware of the ravages that time produces in our poor human bodies. It should be obvious to us that we don't have to reach a hundred years of age in order to recognize the effects of aging in our own minds and bodies.

I was giving a talk recently to an audience of retired persons and I mentioned to them that the aging process usually proceeds gradually but nonetheless relentlessly as the years pile up. I noted my own experience of moving from ordinary eyeglasses to bifocals and then trifocals and that I wondered what would come next. A voice piped up from the audience: "How about cataracts?" This is undoubtedly an example of that "outer nature" to which St. Paul refers and which, though it has usually served us well, will inevitably show the effect of years of wear and tear.

Nonetheless, Paul can assure us with absolute confidence that we need not lose heart. He can make such a daring statement because he knows by faith that we have an "inner nature," which is untouched by the aging process. In fact, it grows ever younger and more vital even as our minds and bodies begin to fail. This inner nature— this spiritual child within us—was given to us at baptism. For in that sacrament we have been born anew and have become truly children of God as well as children of our parents.

This child of God within us is not subject to the natural weaknesses of human mortality. It can only be harmed by persistent sinfulness. By contrast, it is nourished and grows ever stronger as we become more and more like Jesus in our unselfish behavior. In fact, it is this spiritual child within us that is nourished by our reception of the Body and Blood of Jesus in the Eucharist, on condition that we reproduce in our daily lives the unselfish love that is the meaning of that supreme sacrament.

However, we must also note that this spiritual child can easily be neglected and become weak and undernourished. This happens when our religious observance becomes superficial and does not bring about that deep conversion from negativity and griping and self-centeredness to a witness of hope and joy and loving concern which are the signs of the Spirit of Jesus dwelling within us. We hear a great deal today about the neglect of children, and we are rightly appalled by these reports. But we need to ask ourselves honestly whether we too might not be guilty of the neglect of that spiritual child within us that God has entrusted to our care. This child too needs to be nourished by prayer and devotion to loving service.

Sometimes we see older persons, who are frail and perhaps in pain, but are nonetheless almost radiant with the vitality of this spiritual life that they have nourished over the years. The beautiful child within them seems to smile through their wrinkled faces. This is surely what Paul means when he says that our present afflictions can prepare us for "an eternal weight of glory beyond all measure." For this glory is a radiance that reflects the victory of Jesus' resurrection in our bodies even before we die. It is as if the Lord cannot wait to welcome us into the fullness of light and joy in our true heavenly homeland.

Index of Biblical References